30 Herbs for Your Kitchen Garden

Maureen Little

ROBINSON

ROBINSON

First published as The Kitchen Herb Garden in 2012 in Great Britain by Spring Hill, an imprint of How To Books Ltd

This edition published in 2016 by Robinson

A CIP catalogue record for this book
is available from the British Library.

ISBN: 978-1-47212-041-0 (paperback)

Typeset by Mousemat Design Limited
Printed and bound in Great Britain by CPI Mackays
Papers used by Robinson are from well-managed forests and other responsible sources

FSC MIX
Paper from
responsible sources
FSC® C104740

Robinson
is an imprint of
Constable & Robinson Ltd
Carmelite House
50 Victoria Embankment
London EC4Y 0DZ

An Hachette UK Company
www.hachette.co.uk

www.littlebrown.co.uk

How To Books are published by Constable & Robinson, a part of Little, Brown Book Group. We welcome proposals from authors who have first-hand experience of their subjects. Please set out the aims of your book, its target market and its suggested contents in an email to
Nikki.Read@howtobooks.co.uk.

For
Becca and James
The finest daughter and son
any mother could be blessed with

Contents

Acknowledgements

Many wonderful relatives, friends and colleagues have encouraged and inspired me to write this book and I am grateful to all of them – especially those who stoically tasted and commented on my (sometimes bizarre) recipes. I am pleased to say that none suffered any ill-effects! Any mistakes you may find are entirely mine.

Thank you to:

Most importantly, my family: Georg, Becca and James. Without them my life would be as pointless as mint sauce without the mint. To them I give a bouquet of marjoram because they bring me so much joy and happiness.

Everyone at Spring Hill Publishing, especially Giles Lewis and Nikki Read: your continued support and endorsement is a major part of my motivation. To them I offer a bunch of sage because I hold them in such high esteem.

I would also like to say thank you to Miss Smythe-with-an-e who introduced me to the wonder of cooking with herbs all those years ago. I would give her a bunch of parsley because she gave me such useful knowledge.

Introduction

There is much pleasure to be had from growing your own herbs – they are decorative; many, if not all, are aromatic; they attract beneficial insects; and are relatively easy to grow. As if these were not reasons enough to cultivate them, herbs have a variety of practical uses too – indeed, if herbs were people, then in today's parlance they would be 'multi-taskers'! In this book, however, we will be looking at culinary herbs. These are plants which, through generations of use, we know are safe to eat, fresh, dried, or cooked.

Although my dad and mum had a market garden and plant nursery, my first real taste of herbs came about because of my cookery teacher at school. Bear in mind that this was at a time when, in our neck of the woods, even a red pepper was exotic and the nearest you got to a Chinese meal was the new-fangled ready-meal Vesta Chow Mein. Our cookery teacher, Miss Smythe-with-an-e, was looked on as somewhat avant-garde, introducing us to coq au vin instead of chicken casserole, using cos lettuce instead of the limp 'cabbage' type, and – most radical of all – presenting us with a bunch of *fines herbes* (the quintessential French combination of chervil, chives, parsley and tarragon) and using them to make the most sublime omelette I have ever tasted. Goodness only knows where she got those herbs from. She must have grown them herself: at that time the only herbs you could buy were sorry-looking specimens in jars that looked like scrunched-up wheat cereal (you know the kind – the one that even my husband can't eat three of) lurking at the back of the grocer's dry goods shelf.

As a result of Miss Smythe-with-an-e's influence, I pestered my dad to allow me some space in his propagating house to grow some herbs – not always successfully – but I learned enough, mostly through trial, error and effort, to be able to grow some of the better-known herbs like parsley, sage, rosemary and thyme (I feel a song coming on!). The rest, as they say, is history. But whenever I taste an omelette with *fines herbes* I am instantly transported back to the school teaching kitchen

1

and Miss Smythe-with-an-e and her sensible lace-up shoes, baby-pink twin-set and string of pearls, but carrying with her an almost indiscernible, but nevertheless unmistakable, aroma of Chanel No. 5. What with the *fines herbes* and Chanel perfume, us girls often wondered if Miss Smythe-with-an-e's mother was French: the more romantic among us contemplated the possibility of – *bon Dieu* – a French boyfriend! We never did find out, but I shall be eternally grateful to Miss S. for that early introduction to fresh herbs.

This is a seasonal guide but not in the usual sense. Instead of adhering to the usual spring, summer, autumn and winter categories, I have arranged the year into two, key seasons: the dormant season and the growing season. Within each of the two-season classification I have introduced subcategories which I think will prove useful when looking at different jobs to do in the herb garden. These are the early, main and late dormant periods (which roughly correspond to late autumn, winter and early spring), and the early, main and late growing periods (which essentially tally with late spring, summer and early autumn).

There are a number of reasons for dividing the year like this. First, even though we traditionally recognise spring, for example, as being the months of March, April and May, plants are governed by day length and temperature: how many times have we reached Easter only to find the daffodils long gone – or are still enjoying roses in November? Plants start and stop growing according to natural conditions, not an arbitrary date!

Second, the jobs we find ourselves doing in the herb garden are also dependent on what the plants are doing and the prevailing conditions: even though it might tell you on the seed packet to plant out your tender herb in late spring, there is no point doing this until the last frosts have gone. And if seed is ripe in July, don't leave it until September to collect it.

Third, and perhaps most important for this guide, I have divided the culinary herbs that we are going to look at into two main groups – delicate ones and robust ones (which I first referred to in my ebook, *How to Grow Your Own Herbs*). Broadly speaking, delicate herbs are those that we can harvest and use during the growing season; this is when we lean towards fresher, lighter dishes and when we call for corresponding flavours from our herbs. Robust herbs are ones that we can harvest all year round, even in the dormant season. This is when more comforting, substantial recipes requiring longer cooking are the order of the day, the staying power of our robust herbs adding to their flavour. For anyone who has little or no experience of using herbs in their cooking, I hope this distinction will prove to be useful.

Last, even though herbs are available all year round in the supermarket, this book is about encouraging you to grow and use your own. Unless you have sophisticated equipment which provides 'unnatural' heat and light all through the year – like the growers who supply supermarkets – you will be governed by what nature dictates can be grown at any particular time. I guarantee that you would be hard pushed to grow dill, for example, during the dormant season. So you see how a two-season year is practicable when it comes to both growing and using herbs.

I have divided the book into three parts, each one containing two chapters. Part 1 is dedicated to various 'herb' techniques. Chapter 1 is devoted to looking at my selected range of culinary herbs and how to grow them. We also look at where to grow them and how to propagate them. In Chapter 2 we discover when and how to harvest our selected herbs and explore different ways of preserving them.

We look at seasonal jobs in the herb garden in Part 2. Chapter 3 focuses on the growing season. Here you will find what jobs need to be done in the herb garden during the warmer, lighter months. Chapter 4 takes us through the jobs for the dormant season.

In Part 3 the focus is on individual herbs. Chapter 5 covers my range of delicate herbs, with individual entries, providing lots of information on how to grow them, along with recipes for each herb. Chapter 6 contains entries and recipes for the robust herbs.

I have tried to offer recipes that are neither complicated nor call for ingredients that you can't get from a market, grocer or supermarket. And because this book is about making the most of herbs, they take centre stage or have a major supporting role in all the recipes. I hope you enjoy making – and eating! – the dishes as much as I do.

Latin and common name

When talking about plants it is customary to use their Latin names to avoid confusion. On this occasion, however, I have deliberately stuck to the generally accepted English common name of the herbs that we will be looking at. You will find the Latin names in the list of herbs in Appendix 1, however. The reason for using the common name is that when a recipe calls for a herb (or any other vegetable or fruit for that matter), it is invariably referred to by its common name: I can't ever recall being asked to crush two cloves of *Allium sativum* (garlic) to add to my finely chopped *Petroselinum crispum* (parsley)! Where there is more than one common name in widespread usage, I shall endeavour to give the alternatives, too.

Hardiness zone

My experience as a gardener is restricted to the British Isles, so all the recommendations I make and examples I give in this book are based on this. Our climate has been categorised as falling generally within hardiness zone 8a (approximately -9° to -12°) or 8b (approximately -7° to -9°): these correspond roughly to the new Royal Horticultural Society hardiness designations of H5 and H4 respectively. If you are gardening outside the British Isles, adjustments must be made.

Part 1
Techniques

In Part 1 we look at the why, what, where and how of growing my selected herbs, followed by harvesting and preserving. Many of the techniques that we look at also apply to other plants, but I think it is as well to rehearse them with specific reference to herbs. Even if you do have gardening experience, I hope you will still find some inspiration and motivation to take a closer look at herbs.

Chapter 1

The Why, What, Where and How of Growing Herbs

The use of herbs has a long pedigree: herbs were certainly used in worship and ritual ceremonies in ancient Egypt; in China their medicinal qualities were recognised as far back as 3000BC. Exactly when herbs began to be used in cooking, however, is not known; I can't help but think, though, that as soon as Mr Sapiens discovered that, as well as roasting it over a fire, his wild boar could be cooked by boiling it in water in a pot, that Mrs Sapiens chucked a bit of greenstuff in to add some flavour.

I suppose the real milestone came when herbs were grown *on purpose*, rather than just gathered from the hedgerow. In Britain we have evidence that the Romans cultivated gardens around their villas in which herbs as well as other plants were grown. There is no doubt that some of the herbs, such as bay, lovage and coriander found their way into recipes. The most notable example of a Roman garden is at Fishbourne Roman Palace near Chichester in West Sussex – well worth a visit if you are ever down that way. And I wouldn't mind betting that some herbs were grown in a cultivated patch long before the Romans came along.

Although culinary fashions, like many others, come and go, it is inconceivable that there was never a time since before the Roman occupation when someone has not cultivated herbs to use in cooking. From tucking a few chives in a pot to grow by the back door, to formal, well-stocked gardens of stately homes, herbs are very much a part of our gardening and cooking heritage. So let's continue it now by growing some of our own!

Why should I grow and use culinary herbs?

Perhaps I should answer the second part of that question first. My answer would be flavour. There is no doubt that herbs bring another layer of seasoning to almost any dish: they can transform other ingredients by emphasising or complementing their flavour. As for the first part of the question, you could quite justifiably say that there is little point in growing your own herbs when they are now available all year round in the supermarket. This is true. But I think it is worth growing your own herbs for a number of reasons (in no particular order).

First, I grow herbs because I like the seasonality that they bring. I try to use ingredients that are naturally in season in my part of the world, so I wouldn't expect to eat asparagus in December, for example, and the same is true of something like basil.

Second, I like to know *how* and *where* what I eat has been grown: growing my own herbs means that I am in control of what, if any, chemicals are applied to them, and I don't have to resort to buying herbs that have been air-freighted from abroad, and the ecological and ethical dilemmas that come with them.

Third, gram for gram, it is undoubtedly cheaper to grow your own.

Fourth, there is something very, very special – almost spiritual – about planting a seed in the ground, trusting in its germination, and then watching the seedling grow to maturity and harvesting what the plant offers.

Fifth, where I grow my herbs is a beautiful part of the garden with a patchwork of texture and colour.

Sixth, the scent of herbs. There is nothing quite as sensual as brushing past lavender or rosemary on a midsummer's day so that they release their heady, aromatic perfume, or crushing a leaf of lemon verbena between your fingers and being hit with a shot of lemon sherbert.

I hope I have convinced you!

What culinary herbs should I grow?

Ultimately the choice is yours, but there are some herbs that are extremely popular and perhaps these should form the basis of your collection: for example, parsley, sage, rosemary and thyme. There are other common herbs, too, that ought to be on the 'must have' list, like chives, basil, oregano, tarragon and mint. In addition there are some herbs that are not as widely used as the ones I have already mentioned, but are, nonetheless, still worth growing: I am thinking of summer and winter savory, chervil, hyssop and celery leaf, to name but a few. I have selected thirty of my favourite herbs, some of which you might like to include in your collection.

Dividing herbs into groups

It can be a bit confusing when faced with a list of herbs, especially if it is just a straightforward alphabetical one and contains things with which you are not familiar. To make life a little easier I have devised a way of grouping the herbs that not only helps with their cultivation, but also with the way they are used in the kitchen. I call them my 'robust' herbs and my 'delicate' herbs. Let me explain further by looking at my two groups.

What are robust herbs?
Generally speaking the herbs that I call robust are the tough guys of the herb world – they are those evergreen, hardy herbs that make it through the cold, dormant season with little, if any, protection. These herbs, again generally speaking, contain high concentrations of essential oils in the leaves. And, because the leaves are tough enough to withstand extreme temperatures, the essential oils that are tucked away in them are released slowly during the cooking process. So if the recipe calls for long, slow cooking, like a casserole or stew, or if you are roasting anything, you will need a herb that is robust enough to handle this type of cooking – hence the name I have given this group.

You can, of course, use any of the robust herbs in recipes with shorter cooking times, but be aware that the flavour of these herbs can be quite pungent, so the old adage of 'less is more' applies here!

My selected robust herbs are:
    Bay • Celery leaf • Chervil • Garlic • Horseradish • Hyssop
    Lavender • Myrtle • Oregano • Parsley • Rosemary • Sage
    Thyme • Winter savory

What are delicate herbs?

Included in my second group are:

- Annual herbs that germinate, grow and set seed all in one year (like dill).
- Biennial herbs (like parsley): although, in theory, biennial herbs will last for two years – germinating and growing in the first year and flowering and setting seed in the second – we generally grow them for their leaves rather than flowers or seeds, so I grow a new batch each year, sometimes twice a year.
- Non-evergreen, hardy perennials (like mint).
- The more tender or tropical perennials (like tarragon and lemon grass respectively).

All of these herbs require little or no cooking, and indeed will not thank you if they are in contact with heat for any length of time. Always add them to the dish towards the end of the cooking time, preferably the last few minutes. The reason for doing this is because the leaves are quite delicate (that's why I call them my delicate group) and, as a rule, they contain much less essential oil: exposure to heat will reduce the leaves to almost nothing and the delicate flavour will be all but lost.

Given the type of plant groups that my delicate herbs fall into, the list is somewhat longer than for robust herbs.

My selected delicate herbs are:

Basil • Bergamot • Borage • Celery leaf • Chervil • Chives
Coriander • Dill • Fennel • Lemon balm • Lemon grass
Lemon verbena • Lovage • Mint • Parsley • Summer savory
Sweet cicely • Sweet marjoram • Tarragon

Exceptions!

There are always exceptions to the rule and the sharp-eyed among you will have noticed that celery leaf, chervil and parsley are included in both groups. This isn't a mistake – these are hardy biennial herbs, so if you sow seeds late in the growing season and protect the plants with a cloche or horticultural fleece you will have a modest supply of fresh leaves throughout the dormant season.

Where should I grow my herbs?

If you want to grow herbs for cutting they are best grown directly in the ground where they can get their roots down and make strong, abundant growth. You will need to make sure that the soil conditions and situation are suitable for the herbs you are growing.

This is where our grouping comes in handy again. Generally speaking, the herbs in our robust group are those that like free-draining, verging on poor, soil and a very sunny position. A number of these hail from Mediterranean regions, which gives us a clue to the sort of conditions they like. Many of our delicate herbs, however, like a richer soil that can retain a little more moisture, and many can also cope with a little light shade.

If your allocated space is big enough I would advise you to divide it into two sections to accommodate the different groups and requirements – have a look at some of the designs later in the chapter for some ideas.

Soil

One thing that all my chosen herbs have in common is that they like neutral soil. This means that the soil's pH ('potential of Hydrogen') level should be in the range of 6.5 to 7. If you are not sure what pH your soil is, it is worth investing in an inexpensive testing kit from your local garden centre, which will give you a reasonably accurate reading. If your soil is slightly alkaline (this will be indicated by a slightly higher pH number), all is not lost. Most herbs will cope with these conditions. If the reading is lower, it means that your soil is slightly acid, which is a little more problematic. If this is the case, you may need to add some lime to the soil to bring the pH level up.

Preparing the ground

Whatever herbs you are planning to grow, it is worth spending time preparing the ground before you start planting. I think the best time of year to begin preparation is the early dormant season – the reason for this will become clear.

The most important preparation task is to make sure that the area is free of weeds. Annual weeds pose few difficulties – these can be hoed off before they have a chance to set seed, and simply left on the surface of the soil to wither, or be gathered up and put on the compost heap.

Perennial weeds may be more challenging. There are three main ways of dealing with these sorts of weeds: first, if you don't mind using chemicals, you could use a systemic herbicide. This is a weed-killer that you apply to the leaves of the weed. The chemicals are absorbed by the plant through the leaves and taken down to the roots so that the entire plant is killed off. It certainly does the job but you have to be careful not to accidentally get the weed-killer on plants nearby that you don't want to get rid of.

Second, you can dig the weeds up. You have to be careful to get every piece of root out of the ground, though: any left in will sprout and grow. Please don't do what I once saw in a magazine article about ground preparation. There was a picture of a fairly large plot being rotovated: nothing wrong with that, except that what was being chopped up by the rotovator blades was a magnificent crop of young thistles. I had to do a double take. I can't begin to imagine what the plot looked like later in the season when all those tiny pieces of thistle root had had a chance to sprout and grow!

Third, you can cover the area with something that will keep out the light – and then wait. By denying the weeds one of the essential things they need to grow – in this case sunlight – they will perish naturally. Any weeds that do survive will be much weaker and easier to dig out. This method takes a little forward planning, which is why I advocate starting preparing the ground in the early dormant season.

When I am preparing a new bed, I tend to combine methods two and three. I dig out as many weeds as I can but also cover the area with black plastic over the dormant season.

If the herbs you wish to grow are ones that need a reasonably rich soil, it is as well to apply some organic matter such as manure or compost at the preparation stage. Spread it on the soil to a depth of about 5cm, after you have cleared the weeds but before you cover it with black plastic. By the end of the dormant period the worms will have taken the manure or compost down into the heart of the soil and you will be left with a lovely, forkable tilth when you take off the plastic.

To my mind, the soil is more important than the position, so concentrate on getting the soil right and err on the side of a sunny position rather than shade. Most herbs will survive, but not thrive, in shady conditions, so try and avoid a north-facing spot.

I know of no herb that can cope with severe windy conditions, especially if they are exposed to blasts of icy wind during the dormant season. Try and choose a spot that is sheltered, or if this cannot be avoided, erect a wind-break to protect your precious plants from the worst of the weather.

Growing herbs in a herb garden

The *pièce de résistance* for any herb enthusiast is to have a garden solely for the purpose of growing herbs. The size of your garden will depend on how much space you have to spare and how many herbs you are likely to use. Bear in mind that the average spread of most of the common herbs (parsley, sage, oregano, for example) is in the region of 25–45cm: this will give you a rough idea of how many you will be able to fit in your allocated space.

If you are lucky enough to be able to have a separate herb garden, you can make it as formal or as relaxed as you like. Traditionally, herb gardens tend to be quite formal and geometric in design, bounded by a low hedge of clipped box (*Buxus sempervirens*), wall germander (*Teucrium* x *lucidrys*) or similar plants; this contains the sometimes lax growth of some herbs.

Although we habitually call such gardens 'knot' gardens, they are more accurately called parterres. True knot gardens were planted for the intricate hedge patterns alone – different varieties of hedging plants were 'interwoven' in the same design and the spaces between were often filled with coloured gravel. A parterre, on the other hand – from the French *parterres de broderie* (embroidery patterns) – used only one type of hedging and the spaces between were planted with ornamental flowers. What we recognise as a knot garden in the herb sense is really a combination of the true knot garden and the parterre. Either way, if you have the space, there is nothing that quite matches this type of design for a herb garden.

But you don't have to stick with tradition. You can arrange your herbs in whichever way suits you best, and if you find that the design isn't quite as you imagined it, you can always tweak it or move the plants!

Designs for Culinary Herb Gardens

Here are some ideas for three culinary herb garden designs. Each of them contains all thirty of my selected herbs, but, depending on the space you have and your personal preference, you could reduce the number of varieties and have more of your own particular favourites. The plans are just ideas to set you thinking – use them, amend them, play around with them as you wish!

The Traditional Herb Garden

I was very much inspired by traditional designs for herb gardens for this plan. At the centre is a knot design – one without any planting

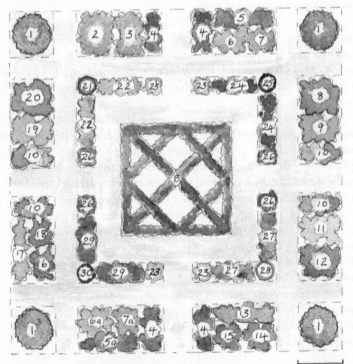

The Traditional Herb Garden   I METRE

14

between the hedges. To make it any more intricate in such a small space would be to lose the 'under and over' effect of the hedge, so I have kept to a very simple design where 'less is more'.

The rest of the garden is divided into beds in which I have grouped robust and delicate herbs together for ease of cultivation.

You will also notice that some herbs are in pots. Three of them are borderline hardy or tender, so I have suggested that they are grown in containers; this way they can be put under cover during the dormant season. The fourth is horseradish, which can be invasive. The other two invasive herbs – mint and lemon balm – have beds of their own so they won't encroach on any other herb.

Although not shown on the plan, the whole garden could be enclosed by a hedge or low wall, with one or two entrances left at strategic points. This would allow a seat or two to be placed at the end of one or more of the cul-de-sac paths, all the better to enjoy the garden.

Key to Traditional Herb Garden

B Box (*Buxus sempervirens* 'Suffruticosa')
1 Bay
2 Lovage
3 Sweet cicely
4 Garlic
5 Celery leaf – sown in early growing season
5a Celery leaf – sown in late growing season
6 Parsley – sown in early growing season
6a Parsley – sown in late growing season
7 Chervil – sown in early growing season
7a Chervil – sown in late growing season
8 Basil
9 Summer savory
10 Chives
11 Dill
12 Coriander
13 Tarragon
14 Fennel
15 Bergamot
16 Hyssop
17 Sage
18 Oregano
19 Sweet marjoram
20 Borage
21 Horseradish, in a pot
22 Mint
23 Rosemary
24 Thyme
25 Myrtle, in a pot
26 Lavender
27 Lemon balm
28 Lemon grass, in a pot
29 Winter savory
30 Lemon verbena, in a pot

The Contemporary Herb Garden

This is a modern take on the Traditional Herb Garden. The formal structure is still there, with intersecting 'hedgelets', but it is not symmetrical. I got the idea from a Mondrian painting – I don't remember what it was called but it was one of his 'composition' works. It seemed to me that it could be reinterpreted as a herb garden with intersecting lines of herbs. And in keeping with the structure, the blocks of herbs are set out in a calculated dimension. This relies on the premise of the Golden Ratio, which centres on the number 1.618, denoted by the Greek letter *phi* (Φ). This number comes about if you

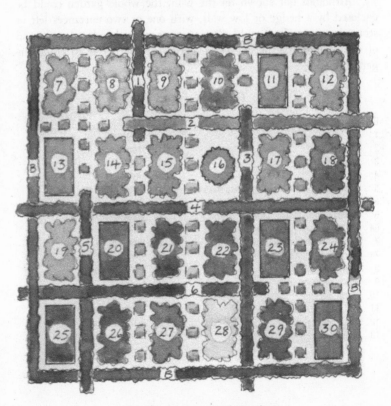

The Contemporary Herb Garden

I METRE

divide a line into two parts so that the longer part divided by the smaller part is also equal to the whole length divided by the longer part. It has long been held that a rectangle whose sides are in the ratio of 1 to Φ has the most pleasing proportions. In my design I have approximated the figure to 1.6, so all my rectangles have the ratio of 1 to 1.6. Stepping stones are laid between the rectangular beds to aid access.

Six herbs are grown in pots – myrtle, lemon grass, lemon verbena, horseradish, mint and lemon balm. The first three are borderline hardy or tender so need to be taken inside over the dormant season; the others can be invasive, so they are kept in bounds by being planted in containers.

Key to Contemporary Herb Garden

B	Box (*Buxus sempervirens* 'Suffruticosa')	16	Bergamot
1	Hyssop	17	Borage
2	Lavender	18	Basil
3	Sage	19	Garlic
4	Oregano	20	Lemon verbena, in a pot
5	Winter savory	21	Lovage
6	Thyme	22	Sweet cicely
7	Summer savory	23	Myrtle, in a pot
8	Rosemary	24	Tarragon
9	Chives	25	Horseradish, in a pot
10	Dill	26	Celery leaf
11	Lemon balm, in a pot	27	Chervil
12	Coriander	28	Parsley
13	Mint, in a pot	29	Fennel
14	Sweet marjoram	30	Lemon grass, in a pot
15	Bay		

The Border Herb Garden

This design is much more informal and relaxed than the previous two, but once again all thirty herbs are catered for. As before, you will notice that some herbs are in pots – these are the usual less hardy or invasive suspects: growing them in containers makes it easier to deal with their special requirements. I have also included a bench – ideal for a sit-down and cuppa when you need a break from the weeding!

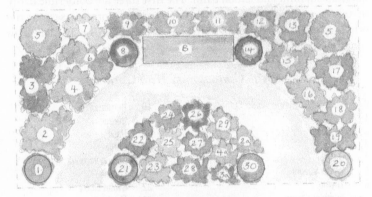

The Border Herb Garden

50 CM

Key to Border Herb Garden

B	Bench	14	Myrtle, in a pot
1	Horseradish, in a pot	15	Chives
2	Parsley – sown in early growing season	16	Sweet marjoram
2a	Parsley – sown in late growing season	17	Tarragon
3	Celery leaf – sown in early growing season	18	Summer savory
3a	Celery leaf – sown in late growing season	19	Basil
4	Chervil – sown in early growing season	20	Lemon grass, in a pot
4a	Chervil – sown in late growing season	21	Lemon balm, in a pot
5	Bay	22	Thyme
6	Coriander	23	Sage
7	Dill	24	Winter savory
8	Lemon verbena, in a pot	25	Rosemary
9	Bergamot	26	Lavender
10	Sweet cicely	27	Hyssop
11	Lovage	28	Garlic
12	Fennel	29	Oregano
13	Borage	30	Mint, in a pot

Growing herbs with other plants

If you don't have room for a special herb garden, you can grow your herbs mixed in with other plants in your garden, provided that the soil conditions are right. Lots of culinary herbs are very decorative and certainly wouldn't look out of place among the roses and delphiniums. I would make sure that you can reach the herbs easily from the edge of the bed, though; you don't want to be trampling over your prize geraniums to get to a sprig of parsley.

Companion planting

One place in the garden where culinary herbs not only look good but are also reputedly beneficial to other plants is in the vegetable plot. Although some of the evidence is empirical rather than scientific, many gardeners maintain that certain plants improve growth and others deter bad bugs or attract good ones. Certain herbs, if left to flower, undoubtedly attract beneficial insects, like bees, which help with pollination of other crops. Such herbs include bergamot, borage, chives, hyssop, lavender, mint, oregano, rosemary, sage, savory, sweet marjoram and thyme.

Whether you believe its premise or not, it's worth giving companion planting a try simply because the pairings often look very attractive. Here are a few combinations to experiment with.

Herb	Companion	Benefits
Basil	Tomatoes	Improves flavour and growth
Basil	Asparagus	Repels asparagus beetle
Borage	Tomatoes/beans/squash	Flowers attract bees for pollination
Chervil	Lettuce/broccoli	Deters aphids
Chives	Roses	Deters black spot and aphids
Chives	Cabbage family	Deters cabbage white butterfly
Dill	Cabbage family	Improves flavour
Garlic	Roses/fruit trees	Deters aphids
Hyssop	Cabbage family	Deters cabbage white butterfly
Mint	Any	Deters ants
Oregano	Tomatoes/peppers	Repels aphids
Rosemary	Carrots	Deters carrot fly
Sage	Cabbage family/carrots	Deters cabbage white butterfly/carrot fly
Savory	Beans	Improves flavour
Thyme	Cabbage family	Deters whitefly

Growing herbs in containers

If you don't have space in the garden you can grow herbs in containers. This way you can position them within easy reach and choose exactly the best spot for them in terms of sun. You can also tailor the compost that you use to suit each herb. Generally speaking, I would use soil-based compost, like John Innes potting compost, rather than a peat-based one: very few herbs grow happily in peat so it doesn't make sense to fill your pots with it. A soil-based compost will also retain moisture much better, which is essential if you grow anything, not just herbs, in pots. Moisture will evaporate far quicker from a container than from open soil and during the growing season your pots will undoubtedly have to be watered every day and sometimes twice a day. As a rough guide, 2.5cm (1 inch) of water will penetrate about 15–20cm (6–8 inches) of soil, so you can see that even if it rains you will still have to top up your containers.

If the herb requires a particularly free-draining soil, add some perlite to the mixture, at a rate of two or three parts compost to one part perlite. (Perlite is a generic term for a naturally occurring siliceous rock which has been heat treated to produce light, sterile granules. It has a neutral pH, which means that it will not affect the acid or alkaline balance of the soil.)

What type of container shall I use?

You can use any type of container, from hand-crafted terracotta pot to a window box to a hanging basket to an old olive oil can. Whatever you use, make sure that there are sufficient drainage holes and that the container isn't so small that it dries out too quickly. Be careful, too, that if you use metal that it doesn't attract so much heat that the roots are scorched.

Suggestions for planting up containers

The combinations of culinary herbs to grow in pots are endless, but 'themed' combinations have a purpose as well as looking good.

- You could plant a classic *bouquet garni* pot – bay, thyme and parsley (see page 191).
- Or a *fines herbes* collection – chives, chervil, parsley and tarragon.

- A collection of *herbes de Provence* – oregano, rosemary, sage and thyme – would look good, too (see page 194).
- How about a 'Scarborough Fair' pot? In other words, parsley, sage, rosemary and thyme! All are useful in no end of recipes.
- Or perhaps a container of herbs for the dormant season? I am thinking of herbs such as thyme, hyssop, winter savory and oregano.
- And a corresponding one for the height of the growing season – basil, summer savory, parsley and chives.
- I once planted a 'Pimms and Pasta' pot, which made a brilliant talking point during a barbecue with friends. I planted up borage and Moroccan mint for the Pimms, with basil and sweet marjoram to go in a tomato sauce for pasta.
- Or you could plant up a container with herbs suited to a particular ingredient:
  - Lamb – parsley, rosemary, mint and thyme
  - Pork – parsley, sage, hyssop and thyme
  - Poultry – parsley, tarragon, rosemary and thyme
  - Sweet dishes – lemon verbena, mint and sweet cicely.
- Alternatively, and for something a little different, you could plant up a hanging basket with herbs: plant chives and purple sage in the top of the basket, with broad-leaved thyme and sweet marjoram around the sides.

How should I grow my herbs?

Before we get to the practical nitty-gritty, I would like to recommend one general method of growing herbs. I would strongly encourage you to grow your herbs organically. For the average gardener, like me, the practice of organic gardening usually means working with nature and what she provides rather than introducing man-made products such as herbicides, pesticides, artificial fertilisers, and the like. I try to dig up or hoe off weeds before they get a root-hold; I attempt to maintain a good ecological balance in my garden so that the ladybirds will eat the aphids and birds will keep the caterpillar population down to a reasonable level; and I feed the soil with a mulch of manure every year.

Although every bit of my garden is run along organic lines, it is especially important to me that whatever I eat from it has been organically grown. Personally, I think my herbs and vegetables taste better, but more crucially, I don't want to ingest any pesticides that the leaves may have absorbed.

The choice of how you grow your herbs is yours, however. Like most things in life, you have to find a way you are comfortable with, which squares with your conscience, but is also realistic and feasible.

Buying potted herbs

If you don't have the time, inclination or equipment to grow your own herbs, there is absolutely nothing wrong with buying herb plants from a garden centre or nursery. The best time to look for them is in the early growing season when new stock arrives almost weekly. Don't be tempted to buy any of the more tender delicate herbs, such as basil, until all risk of frost has passed.

Also, look out for late growing season bargains. Garden centres, especially, sell off herbs quite cheaply at the end of the growing season because they need the space for seasonal promotions. It is really only worth buying the hardy robust herbs, or hardy delicate ones (chives, fennel, lemon balm, lovage, mint and sweet cicely), which will survive the winter. Either plant them in your garden straight away, or repot them and keep them until the beginning of the next growing season and plant them out then.

I would caution against buying potted herbs from supermarkets to plant in the garden. These herbs have been grown under cover, in controlled conditions, and are really only intended to be kept as 'window-sill' herbs. You could try hardening them off (see page 37) before you plant them out, but the few times I have tried this have all been failures.

Labelling

One of most important things to do when you raise your own herbs – or any other plants for that matter – is to keep tabs on exactly what it is that you are growing. There is nothing more frustrating than discovering a tray full of seedlings and having no idea what they are. When they get a little bigger you can often figure out whether they are thyme or savory, for example, but as newly sprungs one seedling looks very much like another. So label everything – every tray, every pot, every row in the garden.

I have some beautiful ceramic herb labels that look especially good in potted herbs. I often give baskets of herbs as presents and the labels make the gifts even more special.

Growing herbs from seed

Some herbs are best grown from seed. In fact, this is the only way to grow annual and biennial herbs like basil and parsley respectively.

Many other herbs can be grown from seed but sometimes germination is erratic or takes a long time – this is especially true of some of our robust herbs, such as bay, lavender or rosemary. I have a rule of thumb that if there is another method of propagating my chosen herb other than by seed – for example, by cuttings, division or layering – I would choose this over and above sowing seed.

Once you have some plants established you can save your own seed, either to create new plants for yourself, or to give away to friends. In order to do this you have to let some of your herbs flower. As well as looking attractive, they will benefit bees and other nectar-loving insects, too.

Collecting seeds

Collecting your own seed is very easy. The best way of deciding when seed is ripe enough to collect is to gently tap the spent flower – if the seed falls away easily then it is time.

Choose a dry, still day and equip yourself with a pair of flower snips or secateurs, and some paper (not plastic) bags or a tray or trays lined with newspaper.

Choose your seedhead and then either shake the seed into a bag or the tray, or snip off the entire head and pop it into the bag or tray to deal with later. Remember to make a note on the bag or tray which herb seed you have collected – you are bound to forget otherwise. (I speak from experience!)

Take your collection of seed indoors and clean it by removing it from the spent flowers and separating it from any chaff or other bits of plant material. Then spread the seed out on a piece of kitchen paper and put it in a dry, airy room for a few days to make sure the seed is completely dry.

Pick over the seed again and remove any damaged ones. Now pop them into a dark glass jar or a stout paper envelope, and label it with the name of the herb and the date on which you harvested the seed. The latter is useful to know because the older some seed becomes, the less viable it is. Parsley seed, for example, is really only viable for a year, but lavender seed will germinate for up to five years after harvesting.

Sowing seeds

Seed sowing can be divided into two main sections: sowing seeds indoors and sowing seeds outdoors. In addition, some seeds can be sown in the late growing season, when conditions for germination are still good – namely, sufficient warmth and daylight – while it is best to wait until the early growing season for others. If you sow seeds in the late growing season, they will need some protection over the dormant period, particularly if the weather is cold. When you buy your herb seeds, check on the packet as to which method is best; or use the chart in Appendix 2.

Sowing seeds indoors

Indoor sowing is suitable for a whole range of herbs that can be started off and grown on inside so that they are already a good size when they are planted out in the garden when the weather is warm enough.

Seeds can be sown into shallow trays, and then when they are big enough to handle they can be transplanted into bigger pots. Or seeds can be sown very thinly into trays with individual modules, which causes less disruption to the root system when you replant them.

Fill your container with compost and gently firm it down. It is best to water at this stage; if you water after you have sown the seed, the water may wash the seed together, especially if it is fine. Scatter the seeds across the surface of the compost and then cover the seeds with perlite or vermiculite, rather than compost. These provide sufficient coverage without staying too moist. Label the container.

Now all you need to do is cover the container with clear polythene, a sheet of glass, or its own plastic cover, and put it somewhere warm. Once the seeds have germinated you can remove the cover so that the seedlings have good ventilation. When they have their first 'true' leaves you can pot them on into individual modules or 9cm pots respectively, depending on whether they started off in trays or modules.

As soon as the plants are big enough, and the risk of frosts has disappeared, you can start hardening them off. This means gradually getting your babies used to the outside world. The easiest way to do this is to begin by putting them outside in a sheltered spot during the day and bringing them back under cover at night. As the plants begin to 'toughen up' you can leave them outside all the time, but you must still give them some protection at night by covering them with some horticultural fleece. The hardening off process should take between two to three weeks, depending on the weather, by which time pesky frosts will be but a memory and the plants will be strong enough to be planted out in the garden.

Sowing seeds outdoors

Many seeds are best sown straight into the soil. Some, like coriander, actually prefer it because they don't like their roots to be disturbed, but check the seed packet to see what is recommended. You can sow seed outdoors as long as the soil is warm and moist, and the air temperature isn't too high, which in practical terms means either early or late in the growing season.

It's vital to have a good seedbed, free of weeds and with a fine tilth (think of the trays that you prepared for sowing indoors). With the corner of a hoe or rake make a drill, or shallow depression, in the soil, the depth of which will depend on the seed you are sowing. Look at the seed packet for this information. There you will also find out how far apart you should sow the seed and space the rows. Then water the drill. Scatter or place the seed evenly along the drill and then cover the seed with a thin layer of soil. Label the row.

You will need to check occasionally if the seeds need any water. If you have sown the seeds too thickly, you may need to thin them out when they are big enough. This simply means removing seedlings so that you are left with single plants, evenly spaced, with enough room between each for them to grow on.

Growing herbs from cuttings

I am an incurable cutting taker. I don't mean that I go around other people's herb gardens pinching off – and pinching – suitable material to use for cuttings; perish the thought. But I do take lots of cuttings from my own herb patch to grow on and give to friends or to donate to charitable events. There are a number of types of cuttings which can be used to increase your stock of herbs: softwood, semi-ripe and root. Have a look at the chart at Appendix 3.

Take heed if you take cuttings, though. Don't expect all your cuttings to 'take', namely to produce new roots and shoots. Some will inevitably die before they have a chance to live, as it were, so don't be disappointed if you lose a good number. I generally take twice as many cuttings as the number of plants I would like to end up with; I usually have a better success rate than that, but I like to be on the safe side.

Softwood cuttings

You can take softwood cuttings in the early growing season. Material is taken from the soft and flexible young shoot tips, which root readily at this time of year. The best time of day to do this is in the morning when the plant is turgid, or full of water. Before you start taking cuttings, make sure that you have a clean, sharp knife and have ready some clean, 9cm pots filled with compost. The number of pots depends on how many cuttings you wish to take: you can fit four or five in a pot.

Select a non-flowering shoot and cut it just above where the leaves join the stem – the node. You need a shoot about 10cm long. Pop the shoots into a plastic bag until you are ready to prepare them for planting: this will prevent them from wilting. When you are ready to plant them, take them out of the plastic bag and, with a sharp knife, cut the bottom of the shoot off to just below a node. Carefully remove the lower leaves and pinch out the top of the shoot. Then make a hole in the pot of compost near to the edge – you can use a dibber, or a pencil, which I find seems to do just as good a job – pop the cutting in so that the first set of leaves is above the surface of the compost, and push the compost back around the cutting. Water the pot from above so that the compost settles around the cutting. Label it.

If you have a heated propagator this is ideal; otherwise pop each pot into a large plastic freezer bag and use the thin paper-coated wire tie to loosely pull the opening together at the top. I don't tie it tightly, but leave a small gap so that a certain amount of air can still circulate. The whole thing then goes on the window sill, and because the pot is inside the bag, you don't need to worry about standing the pot on a saucer. Don't put the pot in direct sunlight, though, as this will scorch the leaves. Open up the bag periodically to aid ventilation and remove any dead or decaying material as you see it. Keep the compost moist.

Once the cuttings are well rooted you can pot them on into their own individual pots. As long as you can do this by mid-summer they will develop enough roots to carry them through the dormant season; otherwise leave them and pot them up early next growing season.

Semi-ripe cuttings

The late growing season and into the early dormant season are the times to take semi-ripe cuttings. These are cuttings from the current season's growth where the base of the cutting is hard while the tip is still soft. The method for taking semi-ripe cuttings is just the same as for softwood cuttings, above.

Root cuttings

You can take root cuttings during the dormant season. First, fill a seed tray with gritty compost, press it down slightly and water it. Then carefully dig up the parent plant, keeping intact as much root as possible. With a sharp knife cut off vigorous roots as close to the crown as you can, but do not remove more than a third of the root system from the parent plant, otherwise it will struggle when you replant it.

Cut each root into lengths of 3–10cm (the thinner the root, the longer the cutting should be), place them on the surface of a prepared tray about 4cm apart, and cover them with a thin layer of compost. Label it. Put in a sheltered position – a cold frame is ideal – and in the following early growing season, when there are signs of growth and the cuttings are well rooted, pot them up individually to grow on.

A friend of mine has adopted another way of taking root cuttings which has proved as successful as any other she has tried. She prepares the cuttings in the usual way, but rather than putting them in seed trays, she simply puts them in a plastic bag with several handfuls of only-just-damp compost. She then gathers the top of the bag together, blows in it so that it is full of air, and then seals it with a wire tie. Then she just leaves it in a cool place until she sees shoots and roots appearing, and then pots up the little plantlets. Easy – and, she maintains, foolproof!

Cuttings in water

One of the easiest methods of making new plants is by stripping off the bottom leaves of a stem – as you would when taking a cutting – and immersing the stripped part in water rather than in compost. Roots will soon start to appear at the nodes (the leaf joints). You should change the water every day to prevent growth of damaging bacteria, and as soon as the roots are about 1cm long you can pot up the new plant.

This method doesn't work with all herbs, but it is certainly a fail-safe way of propagating any of the mints, as well as basil and lemon balm. I have also had limited success with sage, lemon verbena and lemon grass: with the latter you have to make sure that there is some of the woody base left on the stem. Unfortunately my experiments

with rosemary and tarragon were a disaster, but you may be successful
– it's worth a try to get some plants for free!

Layering

Another method of propagation which works for some herbs is
layering. You need a good, strong, established plant for this, and one
that has a tendency to allow some of its stems to droop to the ground.
Herbs that can be propagated in this way are:

Lavender • Mint • Rosemary • Sage • Thyme

The best time to layer a herb is in the early growing season when the
soil is warm. Remove all weeds from where you want your new 'plant'
to grow and dig over the soil so that you have a good tilth. Now take
a long stem from the parent plant, and remove any leaves and side
shoots, taking care not to damage the growing tip. On one side of the
stem, scrape a little of the outer layer away and ease the stem, exposed
side down, to the ground. Now pin the stem in place, so that it is in
contact with the soil, with a piece of wire (I use a piece of cut-up wire
coat-hanger about 15cm long, bent double into a U-shape). Cover the
stem with soil, making sure that the growing tip remains above
ground. Water in well and let nature take its course. Some herbs will
root by the early dormant season, in which case you should sever the
new plant from its parent and pot it up to spend the dormant season
in a cold frame or similar. If the stem has not produced roots by the
early dormant season, leave it until the following year.

Division

Another method of increasing your plant numbers is by division. This
simply means taking an existing plant and splitting it into pieces.
Herbs that can be successfully divided are:

Bergamot • Chives • Fennel • Lemon balm • Lemon grass
Lovage • Mint • Oregano • Tarragon • Thyme

The process of division is straightforward. Carefully dig up the plant,
trying not to damage too many roots, and shake off as much soil as
possible. Then all you have to do is to divide the plant into sections,
making sure that each section has three to five healthy shoots. You
may be able to tease the clumps apart with your hands. Some plants,
however, require something a little more vigorous and you may need

to use a sharp knife to slice the plant into sections. It will become clear as you do it which technique you need to use. Once you have your new clumps you can plant them straight away, making sure you water them in well. If you don't want to plant them in the ground immediately, pot them up individually and keep them until required – again, make sure they are well watered.

Planting out

When the time comes to plant out your herbs – which in practical terms means after the frosts have gone in the early growing season, and before they come again in the late growing season/early dormant season – there is a little bit of preparation to do first. Assuming that the area is weed-free, all you need to do is lightly fork over the soil and dig a hole slightly larger than the size of the pot. If the herb you are planting needs good drainage, put a good layer of horticultural grit in the bottom of the hole and mix some in with the rest of the dug-out soil before backfilling. Firm the plant in and, even if the soil is moist, give it a good watering.

How far apart you plant your herbs depends on their eventual spread, so check this first – too far apart and they look abandoned; too close together and they will become crowded.

How can I keep my herbs growing well and looking good?

Weeding

Try and keep on top of the weeding so that your precious herbs have as little competition as possible. Little and often is the best way, I have found.

Water

I only water my herbs in the garden when I have just planted them and during the first growing season if they are showing signs of stress. Otherwise they have to fend for themselves.

Herbs in containers are a different matter – they require watering at least once a day during the growing season, less often during the dormant season.

Many people maintain that you should only water in the early morning or evening. This is certainly the best practice, but if you see your plants flagging during the middle of the day, water them – by evening it may be too late! If it is a particularly sunny day, avoid splashing water on the leaves, however; water droplets act like little magnifying glasses and the leaves may be scorched.

Feed/mulch

In order to retain moisture, keep weeds down and feed the soil, I mulch at least once a year. This simply means spreading a layer of organic matter, such as compost, on the surface of the soil, taking care not to cover any crowns or soft areas of growth.

If you are growing herbs in containers, you will have to feed your herbs during the main growing season to keep them healthy. A liquid seaweed fertilizer, applied according to the instructions on the bottle, is ideal for this. You could also use a slow-release fertilizer – you can buy this as small round granules – which look a bit like slug eggs when they are incorporated into the mixture – or as compacted 'plugs'. A friend of mine mistook these plugs for bird food – no wonder she gave me a strange look when I added one to my pot of mint! This type of food will last for several months, so the best time to add it to the soil is in the early growing season, especially if you are potting up new plants or repotting established ones.

Prune/cut back

Some herbs will need pruning or cutting back. The idea is to remove any dead growth and to keep your herbs in shape. This helps to prevent disease and to encourage new growth.

Pinch out flowers/dead-head

Unless you want any herb to flower in order to use the flowers themselves, feed beneficial insects, or to set seed, it is a good idea to pinch out the flowering tips of herbs. This means that any energy that would have been directed into producing flowers is now used in building up an abundance of leaves. Similarly, if you have allowed your herbs to flower but do not wish to collect seed, snip off the dead blooms to encourage further growth.

Chapter 2
Harvesting and Preserving Your Herbs

In most cases it is the leaves of herbs that are harvested to use in cooking. Occasionally, however, other parts of the plant are used, such as the flowers, roots and seeds (for example, chives, horseradish and coriander respectively), but before you start experimenting with parts that are not normally used, check to make sure it is safe – your new and exciting concoction may have unfortunate side-effects.

When should I harvest my herbs?

Leaves

If you want to use your herbs immediately, harvest them as and when you need them, but preferably before the plant has flowered, as this is when the flavour in the leaves is most intense. This is certainly the case during the growing season when all herbs are in full leaf. Most of our robust herbs, like rosemary, hyssop, winter savory, bay and thyme, are evergreen and can be harvested all year round.

For soft-stemmed herbs you can use a pair of kitchen scissors but you may find secateurs are needed for some of the woody ones. I use a pair of flower snips that are halfway between the two; these deal with all but the thickest of rosemary sprigs. Never cut more than a third of the growing stems at any one time; although annual herbs, like basil, will grow back fairly quickly, perennial ones like rosemary take more time to recover.

If you cut a few hours or even a couple of days in advance of using the herbs, treat them as you would flowers: re-cut the stems and strip off the lower leaves just before plunging them into a jar or vase of fresh water. Replace the water each day.

If you are harvesting leaves in order to dry or preserve them in some other way, pick them in dry weather after any dew has evaporated but before the heat of the midday sun. Very few of the essential oils will have evaporated and the drying or preserving process will proceed better if there is no moisture on the leaves.

Flowers

There are many herb flowers that can be used in salads, or crystallized to use as decorations. Among them are bergamot, borage, chives and lavender. Like the leaves, you should pick them when the dew has evaporated and before the heat of the sun. To use them, make sure that you separate the flower from any green sepals, which may be bitter and unpalatable.

Seeds

If you want to harvest seeds for use in cooking you should gather them in just the same way as you would if you were collecting them to grow into plants (see page 23). You will have to be more careful at the cleaning stage, however, because you only want to keep the seeds. It is painstaking work, but worth the effort when you can use your own fennel seed, say, in home-made bread.

Seeds that can be used in cooking include celery leaf, coriander, dill, fennel, lovage and sweet cicely.

Roots

Horseradish is the only one among my thirty herbs that is grown solely for its root. This is best harvested after the first frost of the early dormant season, before the top growth has entirely died back. Dig the root either in the morning or the evening: it is at these times when the root contains most flavour. If you leave any bit of root in the ground it will sprout and grow again next year – fine if you want that to happen, but if you don't, you must be careful to remove every trace.

Wash off any soil and the root is then ready to use. Be careful with horseradish because fresh root is very pungent. Some people slice the root into chunks and then dry them, as you would leafy herbs – see below. I have found that freezing the chunks is just as good a method of preserving them. The only thing you have to remember with this method is to wrap each chunk well before you pop it in the freezer, otherwise the aroma will taint other things in close proximity to it. You can also grate it and preserve it in vinegar (see page 35).

Bulbs

The only bulb in my collection of herbs is garlic. It is said that you should plant your cloves of garlic on the shortest day, and harvest them on the longest day. In practice this doesn't always work out. I wait until the foliage starts to turn yellow, then I dig up the bulbs, being careful not to bruise them. Because I can never be certain of having a long spell of dry weather after I have dug them, I take them indoors and lay them on a wire mesh frame that I made for the purpose (simply a square of timber with chicken wire stretched over it). I leave them for three or four weeks and then cut off the dried roots and either plait them, or pop them in a netting bag.

Store the bulbs in a dry, frost-free place. The temperature must not be allowed to rise above 4°C, otherwise the bulbs will start to shoot. Check them periodically to make sure that they haven't turned mouldy or started to rot.

How can I preserve my herbs to use later?

Drying herbs

You might want to dry some herbs. The idea here is to eliminate all the water content. As before, harvest the leaves before the plant has flowered; separate the leaves from the stem and spread them out on a rack made from a piece of muslin that has been stretched over a frame – this allows for good circulation of air. Put the rack in a dark, warm, dry place until the leaves are completely desiccated. Store the leaves in a dark glass jar (to reduce the amount of light getting to the leaves) with a screw top. Dried herbs have a much stronger flavour than fresh, so you don't need as many. Be aware, however, that some leaves with a high water content, like basil and dill, do not dry well.

Freezing herbs

Some herbs can be frozen. Harvest the leaves, and as soon as possible afterwards chop them and pack them into ice cube trays: this is an ideal 'portion' size, which can be used when you have no fresh herbs available.

Crystallising

This method is usually used for preserving flowers, but I have successfully preserved lemon verbena leaves like this too.

The easiest way of crystallising flowers or leaves is to paint them with lightly beaten egg white and then coat them with caster sugar. Leave them to dry on non-stick baking parchment and then store for up to a week in an airtight tin or jar.

Another method, which has a much longer 'use by' date (up to three or four months), is to use rosewater and gum tragacanth, both available from cake decorating suppliers. Mix two tablespoons of rosewater with one teaspoon of gum tragacanth in a lidded jar and leave for twenty-four hours. Then paint the flowers or leaves with the mixture, coat them with caster sugar and leave them to dry, as above. Again, store them in an airtight tin or jar.

Flavoured vinegars, oils, butters, sugars and jellies

Another way of keeping hold of the flavour and essence of your herbs is to infuse them in another medium.

Vinegars

One of the most successful ways of preserving the wonderful flavour of herbs is in vinegar. After much experimentation, I have found that by far the best vinegars to use are white wine vinegar and cider vinegar – these have a reasonably mild flavour compared with the much harsher malt vinegars. They are also more accommodating of the herb flavour that you want to retain. White wine and cider vinegars contain enough acetic acid (5 per cent and 5.5 per cent respectively) to prevent bacteria from surviving, so once bottled, these can be kept for several months. This assumes, of course, that the herbs you use are clean and dry to begin with.

You can make flavoured vinegar with almost any herb, but my favourites are tarragon, rosemary and garlic, and basil and chives.

You simply clean and dry the sprigs of herbs thoroughly (you don't need to chop them) and pop them in a clean, sterilised jar. Top up with your choice of vinegar, making sure that the herbs are submerged, put a vinegar-proof lid on and leave for three or four weeks in a cool, dark place.

Check the vinegar periodically to see if the intensity of flavour is to your liking; then strain the vinegar through a fine sieve and decant into sterilised bottles and seal them with a vinegar-proof lid. Store them in a cool, dark place – they will keep for months. Use the vinegar in salad dressings or marinades.

You can also preserve horseradish in vinegar. Grate the root, put it in a clean, sterilised jam jar, top up with vinegar and pop a vinegar-proof lid on it. Store in a cool, dry place, and whenever a recipe calls for horseradish, simply spoon out the required amount, rinse off the vinegar and there you have it!

Oils

There have been reports about the risk of botulism in flavoured oils. As far as I can tell, this applies more to garlic and chilli in oil than to leafy herbs. However, it is best to take precautions. There are two ways of dealing with this difficulty.

The first is to heat the oil to 180°C before adding it to bone-dry herbs in the bottle or jar. To my mind this is unsatisfactory because the flavour of some herbs (especially delicate ones) will be lost through the heat. And you will have to find jars that can withstand that amount of heat.

The second is safer but is short-term, which somewhat defeats the object of the exercise. With this method you simply mix together all the ingredients – oil and any herbs – pop them in a clean jar, refrigerate it and allow the herbs to marinate for a few days. To be safe, this flavoured oil must be used within a week.

I am inclined to stick with vinegars!

Butters

If you have an excess of any herb, a good way of using it is to make a herb butter. This is very easy to do.

All you need is 125g unsalted butter at room temperature, and about 3 tbsp of your chosen herb, finely chopped. Soften the butter with a fork and gradually incorporate the herbs until they are distributed evenly. Put the butter on a sheet of baking parchment and roll it into a sausage. Twist the ends of the parchment so you end up with a butter 'cracker' and pop it in the fridge for at least twenty-four hours so that the flavour of the herb permeates the butter.

You can also freeze the butter for up to three months; if you do, I would cut it into slices and freeze each slice individually – much easier than trying to cut through frozen butter!

You can use the herb butter to fry vegetables, on grilled meat or fish, in pastry, on savoury scones, in scrambled eggs, on jacket potatoes – the list is almost endless.

Sugars

I love herb sugars. They can be kept almost indefinitely but I find that I use them up in no time at all. You can make flavoured sugar with almost any herb, but I have a few favourites that I keep coming back to. They are lavender, lemon verbena and mint.

The recipe is so simple: all you have to do is to put some caster sugar in a jar (a swing-top jar with rubber seal looks lovely enough to display) pop in some thoroughly dry leaves (lemon verbena or mint) or flowers (lavender), put the lid on, and give the jar a shake. That's it! Allow the herb to infuse for a couple of weeks before you start dipping into it and then use it in place of ordinary sugar in whatever recipe takes your fancy.

Jellies

Jellies are made by boiling strained fruit juice and sugar together to produce a clear, 'bit-free' preserve. Here is a basic recipe for apple jelly that can be transformed into a herb jelly by simply adding some sprigs of your chosen herb to the apples as you cook them, and some chopped herbs to the jelly at the final stage when you remove it from the heat.

Probably the most well-known herb jelly is mint, which is a traditional accompaniment to lamb, but why not try some rosemary jelly for chicken, sage jelly for pork, or even a lavender flower jelly to have instead of jam with your scones?

BASIC APPLE JELLY

INGREDIENTS
2kg cooking apples, or a mixture of cooking apples and crab apples
Approximately 900g granulated sugar
About 6 sprigs of your chosen herb
4tbsp leaves of your chosen herb, finely chopped

METHOD
- Roughly chop the apples, but don't peel or core them. Put them in a pan, cover with 1.2 ltrs of water and bring to the boil. Cover the pan and simmer gently for about 45 minutes, until the apples are very soft and pulpy.
- Tip the contents of the pan into a jelly bag and leave to drip overnight. Don't be tempted to squeeze the bag – the jelly will turn cloudy if you do.
- Measure the strained juice: for every 600ml juice you will need 450g sugar. Put the juice in a preserving pan, bring to the boil and add the correct quantity of sugar.
- Stir until dissolved, then increase the heat and boil rapidly, without stirring, until setting point is reached. (Use a sugar thermometer to get an accurate reading.) Take the pan off the heat and gently remove any scum with a slotted spoon.
- Gently stir in the chopped herb and then pour into sterilised jars and seal.

Part 2

Seasonal Jobs in the Herb Garden

In Part 2 we are looking at the jobs that we can be doing in the herb garden during the growing season and dormant season. For the most part these are the same, universal jobs that you will be carrying out elsewhere in the garden, like mulching, taking cuttings and so forth, but here the emphasis is on looking after our herbs, so there are some jobs that are peculiar to the herb garden, like pinching out flowering shoots.

There are a couple of things that you can do whatever the time of year, however. The first is to keep a journal. Each Christmas my daughter gives me a new notebook. I look forward to this present each year because no two are ever the same: this year it has a bee on the cover. In it I jot down when I sow seeds, when the first frost comes, and so on. I find each one really useful to refer back to in subsequent years.

The second is to enjoy your herbs. Make time, especially at the height of the growing season, to take just a few moments to savour the loveliness of the garden with its olfactory and visual beauty. And even in the depth of the dormant season, marvel at the tenacity of the rosemary as its still fragrant spikes defy the frost and snow.

So, without more ado, let's look at jobs to do.

Chapter 3
The Growing Season

The early growing season

Awake, thou wintry earth —
Fling off thy sadness!
Fair vernal flowers, laugh forth
Your ancient gladness!

THOMAS BLACKBURN, *AN EASTER HYMN*

You can almost hear the new growth stretching towards the light and warmth that the longer days of the equinox and beyond bring. And now is the time for gardeners to limber up and stretch muscles that have been resting all through the dormant season. Although there isn't too much hard physical work to do in the herb garden, there are jobs to be getting on with.

Dig

If you mulched any part of the herb garden with manure at the beginning of the dormant season, now is the time to dig it in. If the dormant season has been particularly mild, you may find that the worms have beaten you to it, in which case a light forking over will be adequate.

Mulch

An additional mulch of compost around some of the perennial herbs will not go amiss, if only to encumber the germination of weed seeds. Be careful, however, not to enrich the soil too much around those herbs that prefer a less fertile soil: I am thinking of the Mediterranean ones, especially, like rosemary and lavender.

Prepare seedbeds

You can also start preparing seedbeds for sowing later. After removing any black polythene that you might have covered the beds with earlier in the year, rake the soil to a fine tilth and cover it with cloches: this will continue to warm the soil and keep it dry, ready for sowing.

Cut back

In addition, you can give evergreen plants a quick trim to keep them in shape. Be careful not to cut back into the old wood of certain plants, especially lavender and sage, because they do not recover well. You can, however, cut back rosemary fairly hard after flowering – it doesn't seem to mind it.

Propagation

Seed sowing

The early growing season is the main time for sowing seeds, both under cover and outdoors. I sow some seeds in the greenhouse, which is not heated. This extra protection benefits some varieties such as bergamot, borage, chives, hyssop, lemon balm, lovage, oregano, rosemary, sage, summer savory, sweet marjoram, thyme and winter savory. You can sow the seeds into shallow trays, and when they are big enough transplant them into pots to grow on until they are ready to be planted in the garden. However, I usually sow the seed into individual modules where they stay until the plants go out into the bed: this method causes less disruption to the root system. Be sure to harden off any plants that have been raised under cover, otherwise the sudden change will be a setback from which they will take some time to recover.

Some seeds have a minimum temperature below which they will not germinate – for basil, for example, it is 13°C, lavender 18°C, and lemon grass 20°C – so I reserve the precious space in my small heated propagator for these.

Later in the season, when the soil has warmed and the temperature has risen, you can sow seeds straight into the garden. As a general rule, the night-time temperature must not fall below 7°C to achieve successful germination and growth. Herb seeds that you can sow outside include borage, celery leaf, chervil, chives, coriander, dill, fennel and parsley.

Cuttings

You can take cuttings of some herbs to increase your stock: during the early part of the growing season, these will be either root cuttings or softwood cuttings.

Root cuttings can be taken from bergamot, horseradish, mint, sweet cicely and tarragon. There are many herbs from which you can take softwood cuttings. These include hyssop, lemon balm, mint, myrtle, oregano and tarragon.

Division

If some of your perennial herbs are getting too big, you can divide them early in the growing season. You can then replace the existing plant with a smaller one and fill in gaps elsewhere in the herb garden, or pot up the divided sections and give them away to friends and neighbours. Herbs that lend themselves to this kind of propagation include lemon balm, lovage, mint, oregano, tarragon, thyme and winter savory.

Layering

You can increase the stock of some of the more 'woody' herbs by layering them. These include the robust herbs lavender, rosemary, sage and thyme, and the delicate one, mint.

Weeding

Make sure you start the season as you intend to continue, and keep on top of the weeds.

Hopefully you will have eradicated perennial weeds before having planted up. If the odd one has managed to go undetected, though, the best way to deal with it is just to dig it up. Judicious mulching where necessary earlier in the year will have prevented many overwintering seeds from germinating, but no matter how hard you try, some weeds will succeed in getting a root-hold. With annual weeds all you need to do is to hoe them off and leave them to dry in the sun or gather them up to put on the compost heap; or you can dig them up. Under no circumstances allow them to set seed. There is a saying, 'one year's seeds leads to seven years' weeds' – how true!

Visit the garden centre/nursery

If you want to buy potted herbs rather than grow your own, towards the end of the early growing season is the time to visit your local garden centre or nursery. By now, strong, healthy new stock will be available. Look out for plants with a root system that fills the pot but is not pot-bound. Knock the plant out of its pot and have a good look – any garden centre or nursery owner worth their salt won't mind you doing this.

The height of the growing season

Hot lavender, mints, savory, marjoram;
... these are flow'rs
Of middle summer ...

WILLIAM SHAKESPEARE, *A WINTER'S TALE*

The herb garden at the height of the growing season! The days are long, the temperature has increased, and often the sun shines long enough for me to tell the time by my sundial, a treasured gift which has pride of place in the centre of my herb garden. My 'sundial times' never quite correspond to TIM (the speaking clock) times because of the longitudinal difference between Greenwich and where I live in Lancashire. I quite like the 'out of sync' time I have in my garden, though: this is my space, and I can do things in my own time, literally.

Every imaginable herb is flourishing and I am spoilt for choice when it comes to deciding which ones should be included in my salad for lunch. Harvest them I must, to make sure that the plants keep producing lots of new, tender, delicious leaves. And unless I want my herbs to produce blooms, I must also pinch out any flower shoots that form, otherwise the leaves become less flavourful and tougher. I do leave some herbs to flower, though – not only do I use them in my cooking, but bees of every kind adore herb flowers.

The growing season is one of the busiest times for the gardener and you may not have as much time to spend looking after your herbs as you would like. Never mind. After all, gardening should be a pleasure, not a chore, so if the herbs look as if they're having a bad hair day, does it really matter?

Weeding

If you do have time, however, there are jobs to do, and one of the major tasks is weeding. If you make it part of your gardening routine it becomes a much less onerous task.

Planting and sowing

The risk of frost has long passed and the soil has warmed up enough to start planting out the delicate herbs that you sowed under cover earlier in the year and which you have been potting on since.

Tender plants

You can also plant out any tender or half-hardy perennial herbs, like lemon grass and lemon verbena, that you have kept under cover during the dormant season.

Sowing

The early growing season is also the time to sow some herbs, such as celery leaf, coriander, chervil and parsley, directly into the ground. You must thin them out, of course, otherwise the growing space will become cramped and the plants will grow leggy and weak, but apart from this, leave them alone and they will give you a bountiful crop with a minimum of effort on your part.

You can continue sowing herb seeds successively throughout the growing season, and this will ensure that you have a good harvest well into the early dormant season and beyond.

Take cuttings

During the growing season and into the early dormant season you can increase your stock of all sorts of herbs by taking softwood cuttings or semi-ripe cuttings. It is a good idea to take cuttings of some of the more delicate herbs, not only to increase stock, but as a safeguard in case you lose your existing plants over the dormant season.

Softwood cuttings

Among the robust herbs that you can take softwood cuttings from are hyssop and oregano. Delicate herbs include lemon balm, mint, sweet marjoram and tarragon.

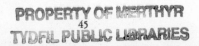

Semi-ripe cuttings

Cuttings from some herbs are best taken as semi-ripe, later in the season. Bay, bergamot, lavender, rosemary, sage, thyme and winter savory are robust herbs that favour this type of propagation. Lemon verbena, one of our delicate herbs, also falls into this category.

Remove flowering shoots

Unless you want some of your herbs to produce blooms, pinch out any flowering shoots as you come across them. By removing them you will divert the plant's energy to producing more leaves. Having said this, I would always encourage you to allow some of your herbs to flower. Not only do they look lovely, they are excellent 'bee plants', providing lots of nectar.

Do some pruning

Some herbs, such as hyssop and rosemary, will benefit from a quick prune to keep them in shape during the growing season; and you can use the prunings as cuttings. Later in the season, after it has finished flowering, lavender will need a tidy-up. It should be pruned every year to keep it nice and compact. When you do this, remove the flower stalks and about 2.5cm of the current year's growth; always leave some current growth because lavender does not regenerate easily from old wood.

The late growing season

*You know the season's progressing
when strawberries and cream
give way to apple pie and custard.*

ANON

How true! There's a transition beginning in the herb garden, too. As the days get shorter and the temperature starts to drop, the delicate herbs are getting past their best; but as long as the thermometer stays above about 5°C, growth is still apparent.

Collect and sow seed

If you allowed some of your herbs to flower during the growing season, now is the time to collect seed from both robust and delicate herbs. A few herb seeds can be sown straight away, which will give them a longer growing period and a head start over similar plants sown in the early growing season, so they will make bigger plants much sooner. Among them are fennel and lovage, and the biennials, celery leaf, chervil and parsley.

Some seeds, like sweet cicely, are best sown late in the growing season because they need a spell of cold to break their dormancy – this is called stratification – and they will germinate at the beginning of the next growing season.

Take cuttings

If you haven't already taken cuttings from some of the more tender herbs, like tarragon and lemon verbena, to make sure you have some plants for next year, don't delay. If we have a mild dormant season, then the current year's plants may well survive, but several good frosts are likely to see them off. Follow the procedure for taking softwood cuttings, but make sure that you keep them indoors, out of the cold, at all stages until next year when they can be planted out in the garden when all signs of frost have gone.

Lift tender plants

Any tender or half-hardy perennial herbs, like lemon grass and lemon verbena, that have been planted out early in the growing season must be lifted and taken indoors before the onset of colder weather. Simply dig them up, pop them in a pot and put them in a frost-free place over the dormant season. They can be replanted outside during the next growing season when all danger of frost has passed.

Visit the garden centre/nursery

You can often grab some late season herb bargains at your local garden centre or nursery. Only buy hardy herbs, and either plant them in the garden straight away or repot them and wait until the beginning of the next growing season to plant them.

Fresh herbs that can be harvested
in the growing season

Leaves

There are no end of herbs that can be harvested during the growing season. Among them are the robust herbs, which are hardy enough to have weathered the dormant season; these include bay, hyssop, myrtle, oregano, sage, thyme and winter savory.

In addition, there are the herbaceous perennials, which having died down over the dormant season, are now throwing up new growth; these include chives, fennel, lemon balm, lovage, mint and sweet cicely. Don't be too eager with the snips or scissors, though – in hairdressing terms, give the plant a trim, rather than a short back and sides when you start gathering a few leaves or stems for the kitchen. Cutting too much, too soon, will do the plant no good at all.

By the height of the growing season, in addition to the robust herbs and perennials in the delicate range already mentioned, you will be harvesting other the delicates: basil, bergamot, borage, celery leaf, chervil, coriander, dill, lemon grass, lemon verbena, parsley, summer savory, sweet marjoram and tarragon.

Flowers

A number of herb flowers can be harvested to use in recipes. These include borage, chives, lavender, dill, fennel, mint and borage. I would be inclined to use them in uncooked dishes, though, as their delicate flavour will be all but lost if you apply much heat to them. There are exceptions, of course: lavender flowers, for example, can be used in baking – lavender scones and biscuits (see page 142) are delicious!

Bulbs

Tradition has it that garlic should be harvested around the time of the summer solstice, but for more accurate information see page 33.

Chapter 4
The Dormant Season

The early dormant season

Where are the songs of Spring: Ay, where are they?
Think not of them, thou hast thy music too ...
The red-breast whistles from a garden croft;
And gathering swallows twitter in the skies.

JOHN KEATS, *ODE TO AUTUMN*

The early part of the dormant season is the time of year when, like the rest of the garden, the herb patch is starting to wind down. The fecundity and exuberance of the growing season is now looking a little dishevelled and drained. There is change in the air as the house martins and swallows line up on the telegraph wires and our resident robin defends his territory with even more gusto, knowing that the leaner, dormant months are not far away. Dawn breaks a little later, evening comes a little sooner, but there are still jobs to do while the mellow days of the early dormant season remain.

Take some cuttings
This is a good time to take root cuttings. This method of propagation suits some herbs like bergamot, horseradish, mint, sweet cicely and tarragon.

Mulch
Mulching can also be done now. The idea of mulching in the early dormant season is to trap the warmth and moisture in the soil. Therefore it is best done before the first frost arrives, but do make sure the ground is not dry – any rain falling after mulching will have another three or four inches to penetrate before it gets to the soil proper and will do little to sustain the plants.

Tidy up

Some people like to leave the main annual tidy-up – removing debris, dead-heading – until much later in the dormant season. The main reasons for this are that spent plant material protects the growing crown of perennial herbs during the coldest part of the year, and overwintering beneficial insects are provided with a home. The main drawbacks with this approach are that the material that might protect the crown can also decay and adversely affect the plants, and homes are provided for 'bad' bugs as well as 'good' ones.

You have to decide which works best for you. Either way, it is advisable to clear away any annual herbs before they set seed, unless you particularly want a natural succession of the same herb in the same place the following year.

Lift horseradish

Now is the time to harvest your horseradish (see page 32).

The depth of the dormant season

In the bleak mid-winter
Frosty wind made moan,
Earth stood hard as iron,
Water like a stone.

CHRISTINA ROSSETTI, *MID-WINTER*

If you are anything like me, the most I want to do in terms of herb gardening at this time of year is to pop out and snip a few sprigs of thyme or rosemary to liven up a warming winter casserole. The days are short and often murky, and by the winter solstice the first frosts have usually arrived and we may even have had some snow. The herb garden doesn't seem to mind the snow that much, though. It acts almost as a blanket, protecting the soil and plants underneath it from dramatic changes in temperature. If we have heavy snow, however, it is as well to brush it off any hedging you may have in the herb garden; the weight of it could damage the structure of the hedge.

Check protection

Check any protection that you have used, like fleece or cloches, to make sure it is still doing its job. Torn fleece or broken glass in a cloche are neither use nor ornament.

Plant garlic

Conditions during the dormant season are hardly conducive to much enthusiastic work outside, and there are few jobs to do even under cover. If the ground is not frozen, one job that you can do, however, is to plant garlic. Tradition has it that the cloves should be planted on the shortest day – around 21 December – and harvested on the longest day – 21 June or thereabouts. Garlic needs a period of cold weather to encourage the plant to 'break' and form a bulb with many cloves. A mild dormant season will not produce the best garlic.

To plant your garlic, make sure the ground is weed-free and rake it over. Gently divide the garlic bulb into separate cloves (don't remove the papery covering) and pop them into the ground, 'flat' end down, so that the pointed end is just below the surface of the soil. Plant your cloves about 10cm apart, with 30cm between the rows.

Review and plan

When all the jobs outside are done, I like to settle myself by the fire with a cup of tea and take stock of my existing herb garden to see if any alterations can be made to improve it. I want my herb garden to be attractive as well as productive.

During the growing season, if I have time, I like to visit gardens around the country and inevitably I am drawn to the herbs. If I see a combination of planting that I particularly like, I take a photograph (with the owner's permission, of course) and tuck it away in a file. When I have the luxury of an afternoon during the colder months I can take these photos out, not only to see if such a combination would work in my own herb garden, but also to relive the memory of that sunny day in July with the scent of lavender and the buzzing of bees ...

As well as collecting photos of other people's herb gardens, I take some of my own throughout the year. This way I can peruse them again and see what has worked well and, perhaps more importantly, what didn't do as well as I had anticipated. It is an odd phenomenon, but you often see details in a photograph that aren't apparent to the naked eye.

I also look forward to browsing the seed catalogues that land on my doormat soon after Christmas. There are always new strains of herbs to try: new varieties of mint and sage seem to proliferate and I can't resist ordering a few packets to see if they are as good as the catalogues would have me believe.

If you don't want to grow from seed you can look through the catalogues or internet sites of herb growers that do mail order. Orders can often be placed during the dormant season and the herbs will be delivered at the optimum time during the growing season – Christmas all over again!

Check preserves

If I have made preserves, such as jellies, from the abundant harvest of herbs earlier in the year, I check to make sure that they are still in good condition. Without opening them, which would break the all-important airtight seal, I discard any that show signs of mould or deterioration. This rarely happens, though, if the preserves have been made correctly.

The late dormant season

Over the land freckled with snow half-thawed
The speculating rooks at their nests cawed
And saw from elm-tops, delicate as flowers of grass,
What we below could not see, Winter pass.

EDWARD THOMAS, *THAW*

Tidy up

If you left some spent flowers and/or stems on perennial herbs, now is the time to cut them back, to allow the fresh young shoots to emerge unimpeded. Also, clear away any other debris that might have blown into the garden over the dormant season.

Prepare the soil

If you are planning to plant out some annual herbs during the growing season you might like to begin preparing the bed. Cover your chosen area with some black polythene, weighting down the edges so it doesn't blow away. There are two advantages in preparing the bed in this way: first, any early weed seeds that may germinate will perish because of lack of light, and second, the soil beneath the polythene will warm up much quicker than if it is left exposed. This will allow you to plant out a little earlier in the growing season – as long as any risk of frost has passed, of course.

Start sowing under cover

Even though the conditions outside may not be right for sowing seeds directly into the ground, you can still gain an advantage by sowing some hardy annual and perennial seeds under cover. These include borage, chives, lovage, oregano, sage, thyme and winter savory.

Fresh herbs that can be harvested in the dormant season

The dormant season is a time of comfort foods: porridge for breakfast, and casseroles, stews and hot puddings for lunch or dinner. This is when the robust herbs come into their own, adding an extra layer of flavour to otherwise modest ingredients like root vegetables and cheaper cuts of meat.

Leaves

Many, if not all, of the robust herbs are still available to harvest during the dormant months: you can rely on bay, hyssop, myrtle, oregano, rosemary, sage and thyme. They will have stopped growing, but they will retain their leaves throughout the season. Even though they may look a little 'moth-eaten' by the late dormant season, they will still be flavourful and will add an appetising fillip to winter dishes.

If grown in a sheltered position, winter savory will also provide some fresh leaves, but it has a tendency to be semi-evergreen if conditions are not too favourable. The biennials chervil and parsley, if you have protected them with a cloche or something similar, will also provide some fresh leaves.

Seeds

During the early part of the dormant season you can collect and dry seeds from celery leaf, coriander, dill, fennel, lovage and sweet cicely to use in cooking.

Other herbs available during the dormant season

This will be limited to your preserved supplies: stored garlic and horseradish, and dried lavender, and any delicate herbs that you might have frozen.

Part 3

Using Herbs in the Kitchen

Part 3 concentrates for the most part on individual herbs – the characteristics of each of my chosen herbs, and how to use them in the kitchen. Classic combinations of herbs, like bouquet garni, are also covered. Again, the groups of herbs are divided into two chapters, one dealing with delicate herbs and the other with my robust selection. In each case the herbs are listed alphabetically, with recipes using each one at the end of the individual entries.

I have assumed some prior knowledge with cooking terms and skills – for example, I don't explain what a marinade is, or how to skin a tomato – but the recipes are not so complicated that you need more than average cooking skills to carry them out. Also, my recipes do not need any 'highfalutin' or hard-to-come-by ingredients that you can't get from a regular market, grocer or supermarket.

As far as equipment goes, you will only need the sort of things that are commonly found in the kitchen of someone who regularly cooks their own meals or does some baking. The only exception may be a mezzaluna and corresponding chopping board: I use a double-handled, single-bladed mezzaluna for chopping my herbs. I have found this to be better than a knife because I have more control over the blade and the end result seems to be more consistent. The choice is yours, though.

All the recipes are for four servings, unless otherwise stated.

The following abbreviations are used:

dsp = dessertspoonful
g = gram
kg = kilogram
ltr = litre
ml = millilitre
tbsp = tablespoonful
tsp = teaspoonful

I give oven temperatures in °C and the equivalent gas mark. If you are using a fan oven, reduce the temperature by 20°C.

So, without more ado, let's get down to the herbs and some recipes.

I hope you will be inspired to try out some of the recipes and, even more important, to compile some of your own.

Chapter 5
Delicate Herbs

Delicate herbs take centre stage in this chapter. There is an entry for each delicate herb – in alphabetical order – which gives information about what type of plant it is and how to grow it, followed by some recipes featuring the herb.

At the end of the chapter you will find some additional recipes using combinations of herbs, and a list of types of ingredients (beef, cheese, vegetables and so on) and suggestions as to which delicate herb goes well with them.

Fresh versus dried

I cannot think of any occasion when I would use any of my delicate herbs in dried form, especially as fresh herbs are so readily available in supermarkets. In contrast to the robust herbs, many of which dry well because they contain abundant essential oil, delicate herbs contain much less and do not dry well as a result. In fact, I would go so far as to say that you might as well sprinkle some stale breadcrumbs over your omelette for all the added flavour you will get.

On the other hand, frozen or freeze-dried delicate herbs can be very useful if you can't get hold of fresh ones. These types of preserving hold on to most of the flavour; be careful not to keep them for too long, however, as they will deteriorate over time. Having said that, I still maintain that fresh is best.

Basil

Ocimum basilicum

Type of plant	Tender annual
Height and spread	45–60cm/30cm
Best position	Sunny, warm site
Soil	Fertile, well drained
Method of propagation	Seed, under cover with bottom heat in the early growing season
Part of plant used	Leaves, flowers

There are many varieties of basil. In one herb catalogue I found no fewer than sixteen different ones! The most common variety, however, is Sweet or Genovese basil (*Ocimum basilicum*). Although it is thought to have arrived in Britain in the mid-1340s, we tend to assume that it is a fairly recent introduction, probably because many of us first came across it while enjoying pasta with pesto sauce on a Mediterranean holiday. Sweet basil is, in fact, the variety used in pesto sauce, a recipe for which is given below.

If you like Thai food you will have come across *Ocimum basilicum* 'Horapha' – Thai basil. Its anise flavour is a quintessential part of Thai and other Southeast Asian cookery. Other notable varieties include Greek basil (*Ocimum basilicum* 'Greek'), which has much smaller leaves than Sweet basil, and Lemon basil (*Ocimum x citriodorum*), which has a delicate lemony flavour and is perfect in salad dressings.

There are also some purple-leaved varieties, which have all the attributes of the green-leaved plants with the added bonus of an unusual colour. Among the best are 'Dark Opal' (*Ocimum basilicum* var. *purpurascens* 'Dark Opal') and 'Red Rubin' (*Ocimum basilicum* var. *purpurascens* 'Red Rubin').

Basil flowers are also good in dressings. Detach a few flowers from the stem and add them to the dressing at the last minute. Or sprinkle the flowers over salads, or as a garnish with summer fruits such as strawberries or peaches.

Because basil is a tender annual it must be grown from seed each year, preferably in a greenhouse. Once all threat of frost has passed it can be planted out in a sheltered, sunny position. Seed can be sown directly outside, but the minimum night temperature has to be above 13°C to ensure germination. It makes an ideal pot plant for the kitchen window sill.

Basil is a good companion plant, repelling white fly and aphids from other plants. It is often grown in the greenhouse alongside tomatoes, with which it has a particular affinity on the plate, as well as in the plot. One of the delights of the growing season is a freshly picked, still warm, sliced tomato sprinkled with torn basil leaves and drizzled with a good olive oil. Here are a few other recipes that include basil.

BASIL PESTO

I have tried several variations of this recipe – one that uses all Parmesan cheese rather than a mixture of cheeses, another with garlic added, but I found that using all Parmesan was a little salty for my taste, and the addition of garlic was just a bit overpowering. Using half Parmesan and half pecorino and no garlic, however, is my favourite combination. As far as method goes, I experimented with chopping the nuts and basil in a food processor, but this resulted in a paste that was too mushy; using a pestle and mortar didn't give me the correct consistency either. My preferred method is now chopping the nuts and basil finely with a very sharp mezzaluna. This way you still get a distinction between the ingredients, rather than them all being amalgamated together in a smooth paste – a bit like the difference between crunchy and smooth peanut butter.

One of the tastiest ways to use pesto is to just fold it into some freshly cooked pasta. I also like to use it instead of the usual tomato base on pizzas: not exactly authentic Italian, but it tastes good nevertheless!

INGREDIENTS
2 tbsp pine nuts
A big bunch of fresh, sweet basil – you will need about
4 handfuls of leaves
25g Parmesan cheese, freshly grated
25g pecorino cheese, finely grated
300ml light olive oil

METHOD
- Dry fry the pine nuts in a pan and allow to cool completely. Using a mezzaluna, chop the nuts finely and put into a bowl.
- Pick the basil leaves off the stems, and again using the mezzaluna, chop them as quickly as possible and put them in the bowl with the nuts.
- Add the grated cheese and stir the ingredients together. Reserving one tablespoon of oil, gradually add enough oil until you have a thick, even consistency.
- Spoon the mixture into a clean, dry jar, pour over the reserved oil and store for up to a week in the refrigerator.

ROASTED PEPPERS WITH BASIL

This is probably one of the simplest, but most delicious, starter dishes ever! It is very easy to make, and the combination of ingredients is almost alchemic. The anchovy melts down almost to a paste, the tomatoes give a real intensity of flavour, and the essence of the basil permeates throughout. You will definitely need some good, chunky bread to mop up the juices!

INGREDIENTS
1 red pepper per person
For each pepper, you will need:
6 basil leaves
2 anchovy fillets
4–6 cherry tomatoes, depending on size, halved
A glug of good-quality olive oil
Black pepper, but no salt – there is enough in the anchovies

METHOD
- Preheat the oven to 200°C, gas mark 6.
- Slice the pepper lengthwise through the stalk. Deseed it, leaving the stalk in place. Place the halved pepper in a roasting dish, cut side up.
- Put three roughly torn basil leaves, followed by one anchovy fillet, in each pepper half. Squeeze in as many halved cherry tomatoes as will fit without breaking the pepper. Grind some black pepper over the tomatoes and finish off with a good glug of olive oil.
- Bake in the oven for about 20 minutes, or until the pepper starts to char and the tomatoes are soft.

BASIL CREAM

I don't think many people would link basil to any sort of dessert, but its peppery flavour goes well with a number of summer fruits, particularly strawberries and peaches. A good way to introduce it to friends and family is as an accompaniment, and this basil cream fits the bill nicely.

INGREDIENTS
150ml double cream
A good handful of fresh basil leaves, roughly chopped
2 tbsp sugar
150ml mascarpone cheese

METHOD
- Put the cream, basil and sugar in a heatproof bowl. Set it over a saucepan of simmering water and stir until the sugar dissolves – do not allow the mixture to boil.
- Remove the bowl from the saucepan and allow the mixture to cool – the longer you leave it, the more pronounced the basil flavour will be. When it's completely cold, strain the mixture through a sieve into a clean bowl.
- Add the mascarpone and whisk until thick but still soft.
- Chill slightly, and serve the same day as you make it.

Bergamot
Monarda didyma

Type of plant	Hardy perennial
Height and spread	60–90cm/45cm
Best position	Sun or dappled shade
Soil	Rich, moist
Method of propagation	Seed, indoors in the early growing season; semi-ripe and root cuttings; division
Part of plant used	Young leaves, flowers

There are a several species of *Monarda* that can be used in cooking, but for looks as well as taste my favourite is *M. didyma*, whose common name is bee balm or red bergamot. It has red flowers with dark red bracts that look lovely scattered on a summer salad.

The minty, slightly spicy leaves can be added to no end of dishes, especially those containing pork, cheese or vegetables, and can be made into a tisane. In fact in North America, where the plant originates, the Native Americans have long used it for medicinal purposes. The early settlers learned about this and named the plant 'Oswego Tea' after the Oswego Native Americans who introduced them to it. The first written account of it by a European is in *Joyfull Newes out of the Newe Founde Worlde*, by a Spanish physician, Nicholas Monardes (hence the plant's name) in the sixteenth century.

My experience with using bergamot in something other than a tisane was limited to say the least, so I set out to concoct a couple of recipes especially for this book. I tried them out on my 'recipe guinea pig' husband who declared them both 'very tasty', so I hope you will like them too.

STUFFED BUTTERNUT SQUASH
WITH BERGAMOT

With bergamot's origins in America, I thought I would marry it with something equally American. Pumpkin pie came to mind. This led to another type of 'pumpkin' – butternut squash – and rather than a pastry case 'pie', I am using the shell of the squash itself to hold the filling. I have used another American (this time South American) ingredient – quinoa – but you can substitute couscous or rice. If you want to go the whole 'American' hog, you can use Monterey Jack cheese, as I do, but any semi-hard cheese will do.

INGREDIENTS
1 butternut squash, halved and deseeded
3 tbsp oil
100g quinoa
1 small onion, finely chopped
1 clove garlic, crushed
6–8 mushrooms, chopped
A handful of pine nuts
1 heaped tbsp young bergamot leaves, chopped (reserve a few for garnish)
100g Monterey Jack cheese, cubed
Salt and pepper

METHOD
- Preheat the oven to 180°C, gas mark 4.
- Brush the halved squash with some of the oil and bake in the oven until tender – about 45–60 minutes.
- Towards the end of the cooking time, cook the quinoa according to the instructions on the pack.
- When the squash is cooked, scoop out the flesh, keeping the 'shells' intact. Mash the flesh and set aside.
- Heat the oil in a pan and gently fry the onion and garlic. Add the mushrooms and cook gently until the moisture from the mushrooms has evaporated. Add the mashed squash, quinoa, herbs, pine nuts, cheese and seasoning, and gently stir.
- Pack the mixture into the shells and return to the oven to heat through – about 15 minutes.
- Remove from the oven, sprinkle with reserved bergamot and serve.

PORK WITH PEACHES AND BERGAMOT

I have cooked pork with peaches before, so rather than reinventing the wheel, I decided to add some bergamot to the sauce and see how it turned out. I think the slightly spicy flavour of the bergamot complements the sweetness of the peaches and honey beautifully.

INGREDIENTS
2 pork tenderloins (about 400g in total)
1 tbsp olive oil
1 medium onion, finely chopped
1 clove garlic, crushed
2 fresh peaches, stones removed, cut into thin wedges
2 tbsp honey
100ml white wine
2 tbsp young bergamot leaves, finely chopped
100ml crème fraîche
Salt and pepper

METHOD
- Cut the pork into slices, about 1.5cm thick. Heat the oil in a pan and cook the pork slices for about 8 minutes, turning once, until they are golden brown and cooked through. Take the pork out of the pan and keep warm.
- Add the onion to the pan and cook for a few minutes, until softened.
- Add the garlic and peach wedges and cook for 3 or 4 minutes.
- Add the honey, wine and bergamot (reserving a little for garnish) and cook gently for a further 5 minutes.
- Stir in the crème fraîche, season, and heat through.
- Pour the sauce over the pork slices and sprinkle with the reserved bergamot.

Borage
Borago officinalis

Type of plant	Hardy annual
Height and spread	45cm/45cm
Best position	Preferably sunny, but dappled shade is tolerated
Soil	Well drained
Method of propagation	Seed, outside in the early growing season
Part of plant used	Flowers, young leaves

Borage is one of the best self-seeders I know, which can be a little annoying if you don't keep on top of the young seedlings; they will inveigle themselves into the tiniest nook and cranny and can be a real nuisance. However, if you can ignore its profligate nature, borage is also one of the best herbs to have in your garden if you want to attract bees.

It's useful in the kitchen, too, since the young, tender leaves – which taste like cucumber – make a lovely addition to a summer salad. Don't worry about the tiny hairs on the leaves – they will dissolve. The blue star-shaped flowers also add a splash of colour to a salad and are *de rigueur* in a Pimms! If you make your own cakes, the crystallized flowers look very pretty as a decoration, especially on individual cupcakes.

Here is a recipe that uses both leaves and flowers, and includes one of the most underrated, and abused (to my mind, at least!) summer vegetables – courgettes. The cucumber-y essence of the borage complements the subtle (some might say bland) flavour of the courgettes beautifully.

WARM COURGETTE SALAD

This calls for small courgettes, the smaller the better – not the 'baby marrows' that are sometimes passed off as courgettes.

INGREDIENTS
500g courgettes
A glug of olive oil
A handful of young borage leaves, chopped
150ml double cream or crème fraîche
A squeeze of lime juice
A dozen or so borage flowers
Salt and pepper

METHOD
- Slice the courgettes diagonally into 1cm chunks. Heat the oil in a pan and cook the courgettes gently, without browning, until they are just tender – don't overcook them.
- Add the borage leaves and cream or crème fraîche and heat through. Stir in the squeeze of lime juice and salt and pepper.
- Serve warm with the borage flowers sprinkled over the top.

Celery leaf

Apium graveolens

Type of plant	Biennial, but usually grown as an annual
Height and spread	30cm/30cm
Best position	Preferably sunny, but dappled shade is tolerated
Soil	Well drained
Method of propagation	Seed, outside in the early growing season
Part of plant used	Leaves and stems in first season; flowers and seeds in second season

Unlike 'normal' celery (*Apium graveolens* var. *dulce*), which is grown for its crunchy stems, celery leaf (*Apium graveolens*) is grown for its – leaves! Celery leaf has been developed from smallage, a herb grown widely in former times for its celery flavour. Smallage had two disadvantages, however; it is poisonous when raw, and extremely bitter. Celery leaf has had this toxicity and bitterness bred out of it, although some people still find it a little too astringent for their palate.

Celery leaf prefers a sunny, warm site, but it will grow in dappled shade as long as the soil is well drained. Although celery leaf is a biennial, most people grow it as an annual because in its second year it will run to seed very quickly. Celery leaf is also known as par-cel because it looks like parsley but tastes like celery. It is invaluable in soups, stews and salads, and, in fact, in any recipe that calls for celery flavouring. It also makes a good substitute for a parsley garnish.

'WALDORF' SOUP

Perhaps one of the most well-known recipes which uses 'normal' celery is the famous Waldorf salad. The combination of celery, walnuts and apples is inspired, so I decided to experiment a little and came up with the following recipe for soup. The apples break down during cooking to thicken the soup and the walnuts add another layer of flavour and texture. I tried making the soup with onions instead of leeks, but there was just too much 'oniony' flavour.

INGREDIENTS
2 medium leeks, cleaned and finely chopped
2 Bramley apples, peeled, cored and chopped
300ml vegetable stock
150ml white wine
1 tbsp sugar
125g walnuts, chopped very finely
A large handful of celery leaves, finely chopped
Salt and pepper

METHOD
- Place the leeks, apples, stock and wine in a pan, bring to the boil, cover and simmer for about 10 minutes, or until just cooked.
- Add the sugar and walnuts and simmer, uncovered, for a further 5 minutes.
- Stir in the celery leaves, season, and serve immediately.

REMOULADE WITH CELERY LEAF

Celeriac is another member of the celery family; it is popular on the continent but hasn't found its way into many British kitchens. Celeriac is a knobbly, bulbous 'root' that looks as if it has landed from outer space, but don't be put off by its appearance; under the misleading exterior is a creamy, flavoursome vegetable that is just lovely made into remoulade. I like to give it another hit of celery flavour by adding some celery leaf – the green of the leaves contrasts well with the cream of the remoulade.

INGREDIENTS

1 celeriac – about 450g in weight
Juice of ½ lemon
4 heaped tbsp good-quality mayonnaise
2 tbsp Dijon mustard (it has to be a mild mustard – not the fiery English mustard)
2 tbsp double cream or crème fraîche
2 tbsp celery leaf, chopped
Salt and pepper

METHOD

- Peel and shred the celeriac. Don't make the shreds too fine or too chunky – you want a 'crunch' to your remoulade without it being sloppy or too chewy.
- In a mixing bowl, combine the celeriac and lemon juice, making sure that the celeriac is thoroughly coated to prevent it from discolouring. Cover the bowl with plastic wrap and refrigerate for about 30 minutes.
- Meanwhile, mix together the mayonnaise, mustard, cream or crème fraîche, herbs and seasoning.
- Remove the celeriac from the refrigerator and drain off any excess lemon juice. Fold the mayonnaise mixture in to the celeriac and serve.

Chervil
Anthriscus cerefolium

Type of plant	Biennial, but grown as hardy annual
Height and spread	60cm/30cm
Best position	Partial shade
Soil	Fertile, moist, but not waterlogged
Method of propagation	Seed, sown outside in the early growing season, or in the late growing season for winter use. Always use fresh seed.
Part of plant used	Leaves

A native of the Middle East and Western Asia, chervil was known in Britain before the year 1000 and was probably brought to our shores by the Romans. It looks quite similar to Italian (flat-leaved) parsley, but it has a very different flavour, with a slight hint of aniseed. John Gerard, the Elizabethan physician, wrote in his *Herbal* of 1597 that 'the leaves of sweet chervil are exceeding good, wholesome and pleasant among other salad herbs'.

It is best grown in partial or dappled shade, either in the open ground or in containers, provided it is adequately watered. It is not a sun-worshipper and will rapidly run to seed if the conditions are too hot or dry. If you want leaves over the dormant season, sow seed in the late growing season and protect the plants with a cloche or horticultural fleece.

Chervil is widely used in French cookery, being one of the ingredients of *fines herbes*. It is also commonly used in a number of dishes cooked during the Christian period of Lent; the recipe below comes from my husband's Tante (Aunt) Doris in Germany, where Maundy Thursday is known as *Gründonnerstag* – 'green Thursday'. It is thought that *grün* actually derives from *greinen*, meaning to whine or whimper, but the colour association has stuck, and green-coloured foods are often eaten on Maundy Thursday.

Tante Doris always serves this soup with her home-made *Sonnenblumenbrot* (sunflower seed bread), the nutty flavour and texture of which complements the soup beautifully.

CHERVIL SOUP

INGREDIENTS

1 tbsp vegetable oil
2 stalks celery, chopped
1 leek, chopped
1 onion, chopped
1 small potato, peeled and cubed
1ltr vegetable stock
A good handful of chopped chervil leaves
Salt and pepper

METHOD

- Heat the oil in a large saucepan. Add the celery, leek and onion and cook gently for about 10 minutes – do not allow them to brown.
- Add the potato and stock, bring to the boil and then cover the pan and simmer until the vegetables are tender – about 25 minutes.
- Take the pan off the heat and add the chervil, keeping some aside for garnish.
- Whizz in a food processor and serve immediately, topped with a sprinkling of chervil.

CHERVIL VINAIGRETTE

Chervil works well in so many recipes, but one of my favourite ways of using it is in a simple vinaigrette. This makes a wonderful accompaniment to salads, particularly if they contain fish or chicken.

INGREDIENTS
Leaves from a large bunch of chervil
100ml light olive oil
1 tbsp lemon juice
Salt and pepper

METHOD
- If you have a food processor, simply whizz the chervil leaves together with a little of the oil until smooth. Add the rest of the oil a little at a time, and then the lemon juice, salt and pepper.
- If you don't have a processor, chop the chervil very finely and set aside. Whisk the oil and lemon juice together until amalgamated, then add the chervil and salt and pepper.

Chives

Allium schoenoprasum

Type of plant	Hardy perennial
Height and spread	20–30cm/30cm
Best position	Preferably sunny, but dappled shade is tolerated
Soil	Rich, moist
Method of propagation	Seed, outside in the early growing season; division, early growing season or early dormant season
Part of plant used	Leaves and flowers

This herb, a member of the onion family, can be found growing wild in Europe, Asia and North America. Although chives have been gathered from the wild since antiquity, it seems probable that they weren't cultivated until the middle ages.

Chives like rich, moist soil which must not be allowed to dry out during the growing season. They love a warm, sunny position, but will tolerate dappled shade. They can also be grown in a container, but should be divided in the early growing season or the early dormant season if the pot gets overcrowded.

It is mainly the leaves that are used in the kitchen, so the flower buds are usually removed. The pink, 'drumstick' flowers are edible, however, and taste – and look – good divided into florets in a summer salad; they are also brilliant for bees. Along with parsley, this is probably one of the best-known herbs in the kitchen. Coming from the allium family, chives do have an 'oniony' smell and taste, although it is very mild. They are indispensable as a garnish and are one of the ingredients of the French *fines herbes*.

There are other varieties of chives that are useful in the kitchen, especially garlic chives (*Allium tuberosum*), which as the name suggests have a mild garlic flavour, and Welsh onions (*Allium fistulosum*), which are more robust than ordinary chives and have larger leaves.

FOUR ONION TART

This recipe combines a number of 'onions' – it's delicious served cold, in slices, as a summer lunch, or if you make individual tartlets, as a warm starter. I use shallots rather than large onions because they have a more subtle flavour which won't overpower the different types of chives. I also like the very slight tanginess of a mild, hard goat's cheese, but you can use any other mild cheese that you like.

INGREDIENTS
400g shortcrust pastry
1 tbsp olive oil
8 shallots, finely chopped
250ml single cream
200ml milk
2 egg yolks
1 egg
100g mild, hard goat's cheese, broken into small chunks
3 tbsp garlic chives, sliced
3 tbsp Welsh onions, thinly sliced
A good handful of chives, chopped

METHOD
- You will need four individual flan or quiche tins or one large flan tin 23cm in diameter.
- Roll out the pastry and line the flan or quiche tins. Preheat the oven to 170°C, gas mark 3.
- Heat the oil in a pan and gently fry the shallots until soft but not brown. Remove from the heat and allow to cool slightly.
- In a large bowl, whisk together the cream, milk, egg yolks and egg.
- Spread the cheese and cooked shallot over the bottom of the pastry case and scatter over the garlic chives, Welsh onions and chives. Carefully pour the cream mixture over the contents of the pastry case.
- Bake for about 30–40 minutes, until the mixture is just set – there should be a very slight wobble in the centre.
- Serve warm or cold, with a salad.

CORIANDER

Coriandrum sativum

Type of plant	Hardy annual
Height and spread	30–60cm/30cm
Best position	Sun for seed production, light shade for leaves
Soil	Well drained but moisture retentive
Method of propagation	Seed sown outside in the early growing season
Part of plant used	Leaves and seeds

Although coriander is native to the eastern Mediterranean it quickly spread to southern Europe, and the Middle and Far East, and can now be found all over the world. Coriander is an ancient culinary herb: the Chinese used the seeds for flavouring more than 5,000 years ago, and it is mentioned in the Old Testament. Both the leaves and seeds were commonly used in cookery in Britain from the Roman to the Elizabethan times, but it fell out of fashion until the last century and the rise in popularity of Indian and Caribbean cuisine.

If you grow coriander for its leaves, the best position is light shade. A combination of sun and too little water will quickly result in it running to seed. For a good supply of leaves, sow the seed in succession from the early growing season through the main growing season.

Coriander leaves are a mainstay of almost every Asian dish, but don't add them too early to a cooked dish as they quickly lose their flavour when heated. There are so many recipes in which you can use coriander – here are a couple of my favourites.

CORIANDER AND MINT CHUTNEY

This is like a traditional Indian chutney. It makes a refreshing accompaniment, especially to fish. It is also very good as a coating for fish baked in foil or parchment: spread it over the surface of the fillets before you wrap and bake them.

You will see that the recipe calls for a pinch of sugar and ground coriander. The other day I discovered that a 'dash' is ⅛th of a teaspoon; a 'pinch' is ⅟₁₆th of a teaspoon; and a 'smidgen' is ⅟₃₂nd of a teaspoon – you can get dinky measuring spoons in the amounts! I rather like the idea of knowing what a smidgen is!

INGREDIENTS
50g desiccated coconut
2 cloves garlic, crushed
2 large green chillis, deseeded and finely chopped
1 large bunch of coriander
1 large bunch of mint
Pinch caster sugar
Pinch ground coriander
Juice of ½ lime
Salt

METHOD
- This recipe is so simple to make it barely needs instructions! Put all the ingredients into a food processor and pulse to a coarse paste.
- If you don't have a processor, you can use a large pestle and mortar – it will take a little longer but the result will be the same.

ROASTED CARROT AND CORIANDER SOUP

There are many variations of this delicious soup – the combination of sweet carrots and the spiciness of coriander is a winner every time. I have added an extra subtle layer of flavour by roasting the carrots first.

You can use ordinary orange carrots for this soup, but yellow carrots, if you can get them, are even better because they have such a sweet flavour, which is intensified even further as you roast them.

INGREDIENTS
2 tbsp olive oil
450g carrots, cleaned and cut into chunks
1 large onion, peeled and chopped
2 small potatoes, peeled and cut into chunks
5 cloves garlic, peeled
1.5ltrs vegetable stock
Leaves of 1 large bunch of coriander
100ml single cream
Salt and pepper
A little chopped parsley for garnish

METHOD
- Preheat the oven to 220°C, gas mark 7.
- Toss the vegetables in the oil and season. Spread them out in a large roasting tin with the garlic. Roast until golden but not charred, turning occasionally. This will take up to an hour.
- Transfer the vegetables to a pan, add the stock and bring to the boil. Cover and simmer for about 20 minutes until the carrots are very soft.
- Take off the heat, add the coriander leaves (reserve some for garnish) and blend until smooth.
- Return the soup to the pan, add most of the cream (reserve a little for garnish), and reheat, taking care not to let it boil.
- Ladle into individual bowls and swirl a little of the reserved cream in the centre of each serving. Sprinkle each with a little coriander and parsley.

TROPICAL FRUIT WITH CORIANDER

Coriander isn't usually associated with sweet dishes, but the acidity of the pineapple is countered by the coriander beautifully. The addition of mango also provides a smoothness to mingle with the other textures. And the recipe is simplicity itself.

INGREDIENTS
1 fresh pineapple
1 fresh mango
2 tbsp fresh coriander leaves, finely chopped

METHOD
- Peel and core/stone the pineapple and mango. Cut each into even chunks, reserving as much juice as possible.
- Simply mix all the ingredients together in a pretty bowl, and serve. I said it was easy!

Dill

Anethum graveolens

Type of plant	Annual
Height and spread	90cm/30cm
Best position	Sunny
Soil	Well drained
Method of propagation	Seed, outdoors in the early growing season
Part of plant used	Leaves, seeds

Dill originated in southern Europe, the Middle East or western Asia, depending on which book you read! Suffice it to say that dill can now be found throughout the world and has naturalised in many areas. It was certainly used, and highly regarded, by the ancient Greeks and Romans, and it is mentioned in St Matthew's Gospel as being used to pay tithes.

Dill is easily grown from seed, but does not like being transplanted, so sow it where you want it to grow. Although it is hardy it appreciates a sunny position with some shelter from the wind. Its feathery leaves resemble fennel but its flavour is quite different: dill has a mild, warm flavour, while fennel has an aniseed taste.

Dill is not often found in Mediterranean dishes but is widely used in Scandinavia and northern, central and eastern Europe. It has a wonderful affinity with almost all fish dishes, especially salmon. It also goes well with summer vegetables such as beans, courgettes, tender young spinach leaves and cucumber. If you use it in a cooked dish, add it towards the end of the cooking time as it loses its aroma and flavour if heated for too long.

GRAVADLAX

Salmon and dill must be one of the most well-known pairings in fish cookery, and in this recipe the two bring out the best in one another in the Scandinavian dish of gravadlax. No heat is required in its preparation – this dish 'cooks' itself, or rather, the combination of salt and sugar 'cures' it.

INGREDIENTS
2 pieces fresh salmon, roughly the same size, boned but not skinned
For each kg of salmon you will need:
5 tbsp sugar (soft brown is best)
5 tbsp sea salt
1 tsp black pepper
A big bunch of fresh dill – don't skimp

METHOD
- Mix together the sugar, salt and pepper. Rub into the flesh side of each piece of salmon.
- Put a layer of dill fronds in the bottom of a shallow dish and place one of the pieces of fish, skin side down, on the dill. Cover this piece of fish with more dill and lay the other piece of fish on it, skin side up, to form a 'dill sandwich'. Cover with any remaining salt mixture and dill.
- Cover the fish with clingfilm and put a small tray or chopping board, roughly the same size as the salmon, but smaller than the dish, on top of the salmon and weigh it down. Tins of baked beans or tomatoes are ideal.
- Refrigerate for two days, turning the fish over once.
- Take the fish out of the dish and scrape off the marinade. Slice the fish as you would smoked salmon, across the grain, and serve.

BROAD BEAN, SAFFRON AND DILL PILAFF

Removing the skins from the beans may seem fiddly, but it is well worth the effort because the 'beanlets' are really tender and succulent.

INGREDIENTS
350g broad beans (shelled weight)
45g butter
1 onion, finely chopped
2 cloves garlic, finely chopped
400g long grain rice
750ml vegetable stock
A pinch of saffron threads
Salt and pepper
3 tbsp chopped dill

METHOD
- Put the beans into a pan of boiling water and simmer for just 1 minute. Drain and slit open each bean to squeeze out the inside. Discard the skins.
- Melt the butter in a saucepan and gently fry the onion and garlic.
- Add the rice and stir, making sure to coat each grain with the butter.
- Add the stock, saffron, salt and pepper and bring up to the boil. Stir in the beans, cover tightly and reduce the heat right down. Cook for 10 minutes.
- Remove from the heat. All the liquid should have been absorbed and the rice tender.
- Add the dill and serve.

Fennel
Foeniculum vulgare

Type of plant	Hardy perennial
Height and spread	Up to 1.5m/45cm
Best position	Sun
Soil	Fertile, moist but well drained
Method of propagation	Seed, outdoors in the early growing season
Part of plant used	Leaves, flowers, seeds

Fennel grown for its leaves, flowers and seeds (*Foeniculum vulgare*) should not be confused with Florence fennel (*Foeniculum vulgare* var. *dulce*) primarily grown for its bulbous root, although you can also use its feathery leaves. Fennel is native to southern Europe and was widely cultivated by the Romans, who used it so extensively in their cooking that few meats were served without some form of fennel marinade or sauce. Folklore has it that if you hang a bunch of fennel above your door on Midsummer's Eve then you will be protected from enchantment and witches.

Fennel likes moist, fertile soil and a sunny position. It looks magnificent if grown in a herbaceous border where its feathery leaves make a superb foil for more robust specimens. Do not grow it near dill, as they will hybridise and their offspring are of no value either as herbs or ornamentals.

In English cookery fennel is traditionally used with fish while in Italy it is married with pork and sausages; there are recipes for both below. You can add the flowers to a summer salad and the dried seeds can be stored and used in sauces or sprinkled on bread dough before it is baked.

SAUSAGE AND FENNEL MEATBALLS

If you are tired of straightforward grilled sausages, this recipe makes a tasty change – and it's very easy. Serve the meatballs with spaghetti or tagliatelle and home-made tomato sauce.

INGREDIENTS
8 good-quality pork sausages (or 500g pork sausagemeat)
1 tbsp chopped fennel
A smidgen of fennel seeds, crushed
Oil for frying

METHOD
- Cut the skins off the sausages and put the meat into a bowl.
- Mix in the chopped fennel and crushed seeds and shape the sausagemeat into small balls – you should aim for about 24.
- Heat the oil in a frying pan and cook the meatballs, turning them occasionally, until they are golden brown and cooked all the way through.
- Serve with pasta and tomato sauce.

BAKED MACKEREL WITH FENNEL

You can use just about any fish in this dish, but I find the aniseed flavour of the fennel marries perfectly with the oiliness of the mackerel. You can bake it in the oven or grill it on the barbecue – if you are lucky enough to get barbecue-worthy weather!

INGREDIENTS
4 whole mackerel, gutted and cleaned
A little oil
½ tsp fennel seeds
2 cloves garlic
4 spring onions, finely chopped
Grated zest of 1 lemon
12 fennel fronds

METHOD
- Preheat the oven to 200°C, gas mark 6.
- Take four sheets of foil, each large enough to accommodate a fish, and brush with the oil.
- In a pestle and mortar, crush the fennel seeds and garlic into a paste. Spread the paste inside the cavity of each fish, along with the spring onions and lemon zest.
- Lay three fennel fronds in each cavity and fold the foil to make a parcel.
- Bake in the oven or on the barbecue for about 20 minutes or until the fish is cooked.

85

Lemon balm
Melissa officinalis

Type of plant	Hardy perennial
Height and spread	60cm/50cm
Best position	Preferably sunny, but dappled shade is tolerated
Soil	Moisture retentive, but not waterlogged
Method of propagation	Seed, indoors in the early growing season; softwood cuttings; division
Part of plant used	Leaves

Lemon balm is native to southern Europe and has been cultivated for over 2,000 years; it was brought to Britain by the Romans. *Melissa* is the Greek word for honey bee, and the plant has long been associated with bee-keeping. Not only is it a rich source of nectar, but Virgil (70–19BC) noted that balm induces swarming, while in the sixteenth century the herbalist John Gerard wrote: 'The hives of bees being rubbed with the leaves of balm causeth the bees to keep together and causeth others to come with them.'

Lemon balm is not as fussy as some herbs and will grow in both sun and dappled shade. It prefers moisture-retentive soil but will not tolerate permanently wet feet. As well as the green-leaved variety there is a variegated form which has splashes of yellow, and sometimes white, on the leaves: it is slightly (but only slightly) less invasive than the all-green variety.

As its name implies, lemon balm has a wonderful citrus aroma and associates well with chicken, fish and vegetables. It also goes well with fruit desserts, particularly apple and rhubarb.

One of the most versatile ways I have come across of using lemon balm in fish recipes is as a pesto. Because fish needs very little cooking time, the essential flavour of the lemon balm is retained. Simply smear the pesto on the fish before baking or grilling and there you have it! Delicious.

LEMON BALM PESTO

The ingredients and method are exactly the same as for basil pesto (see page 60), except that you use lemon balm leaves instead of basil. To add an extra lemon hit, you can include the grated zest of half a lemon.

LEMON BALM AND APPLE CAKE

I've taken inspiration from Greek baklava and Austrian strudel pastries for this recipe, which combines lemon balm, lemon and honey. It makes a delicious dessert or tea pastry.

INGREDIENTS

2 large cooking apples, peeled and cored
Juice of ½ lemon
200g ground almonds
50g icing sugar, plus a little extra to serve
2 tbsp runny honey
A pinch each of ground cinnamon and ground cloves,
plus a little extra to serve
A handful of lemon balm leaves, finely chopped,
plus a few extra to serve
Grated zest of 1 lemon
75g unsalted butter
8 large sheets filo pastry

METHOD

- Preheat the oven to 200°C, gas mark 6.
- Grate the apple into a bowl containing the lemon juice and mix together – this will prevent the apple from going brown.
- Add the almonds to the bowl containing the apple and lemon juice, together with the icing sugar, honey, cinnamon, cloves, lemon balm and lemon rind.
- Melt 50g of butter and stir into this mixture. Divide into three roughly even portions.
- Melt the remaining butter and lightly brush the inside of a loose-bottomed cake tin. Place a sheet of filo pastry in the bottom of the tin, folding over the edges of the pastry to fit the tin if necessary. Brush with butter, and place another sheet of filo pastry on the top.
- Spread one of the portions of the nut and apple mixture over the pastry. Then continue to layer two sheets of pastry (brushing each with butter) with a portion of the nut and apple mixture. Brush the final layer of pastry with butter.
- Bake for 35–40 minutes, until golden brown. Remove from the tin and allow to cool. Dust with icing sugar, cloves and cinnamon.

Lemon grass
Cymbopogon citratus

Type of plant	Tender perennial
Height and spread	30–45cm/20cm
Best position	Sunny
Soil	Well drained
Method of propagation	Seed, indoors in the early growing season; division
Part of plant used	Leaves and stems

Unlike many hardy herbs that we grow, lemon grass is a real softie, requiring a minimum night temperature of 8°C. You could grow it outside in the UK, but it would have to be dug up, potted, and brought in to a heated environment over the dormant season. Bearing this in mind, it is as well to grow it in a container from the beginning. Use loam-based compost and repot early in the growing season if necessary.

It is a mainstay in many Asian, particularly Thai dishes, imparting a subtle citrus-type flavour. Why not just use lemons? Apparently, although a type of lime will grow happily in tropical climates, lemons will not – hence the use of lemon grass. Although the young leaves impart some lemon flavour, it is the bottom 10cm or so of the bulbous stem that contains most aromatic oil.

There are dozens, if not hundreds, of recipes for Thai salads and soups that contain lemon grass, so I am bucking the trend a little by giving a recipe for non-Thai crab cakes, and a sweet recipe using rhubarb, honey and lemon grass.

CRAB CAKES WITH LEMON GRASS

Instead of leaving the crab cakes 'naked', you could give them a coat of breadcrumbs before you fry them – either way is delicious.

INGREDIENTS
500g white and brown crab meat – use fresh if you can get it, but tinned is just as good
1 stalk lemon grass
1 chilli, deseeded and chopped finely
2 spring onions, chopped finely
A handful of coriander, chopped
Zest and juice of 1 lime
100g fresh breadcrumbs – I like to use wholemeal, but white will do
1 egg, lightly beaten
2 tbsp oil

METHOD
- Put the crab meat in a bowl.
- Peel off two or more of the toughest outer layers of the lemon grass stalk, and discard them. Very finely chop the rest of the lemon grass.
- Add the chopped chilli and spring onions, along with the lemon grass and chopped coriander, to the crab meat. Add the lime zest, juice and breadcrumbs, and bind together with the beaten egg.
- Take a small palm-full of the mixture and form it into a cake shape in your hand. Do this until you have used all the mixture. Then put the cakes in the refrigerator for 30 minutes or so.
- Heat the oil in a frying pan and gently lay each cake in the pan. Cook for 6–8 minutes; don't push them around too much in the pan or they might start to disintegrate. Then turn them over and cook for a further 6–8 minutes until golden brown.
- You could serve these crab cakes with the coriander and mint chutney (see page 77).

RHUBARB, HONEY AND LEMON GRASS FOOL

This recipe would work equally well with other fruit, such as apples or gooseberries, but I like to use rhubarb because of its 'candy pink' colour.

INGREDIENTS
700g rhubarb
2 stalks lemon grass
100ml water
50g honey
110g icing sugar
150ml mascarpone cheese
1 small carton crème fraîche

METHOD
- Peel off two or more of the toughest outer layers of the lemon grass and discard them. Very finely chop the rest of the lemon grass almost to a powder.
- Wash and trim but do not peel the rhubarb. Cut into even chunks about 2cm long and put into a pan with the water, honey and lemon grass. Cover and simmer until the rhubarb softens and breaks down – about 10 minutes.
- Strain through a sieve, reserving all the juice, and allow the rhubarb to cool down.
- Return the juice to the pan and reduce gently until it is syrupy. Allow to cool.
- Whisk the icing sugar into the mascarpone, then gently fold in the crème fraîche and half the rhubarb.
- Divide the remaining rhubarb among four dishes and spoon the fool mixture on top. Allow to set and cool in the fridge. When it is time to serve them, drizzle a little of the reserved syrup over the top of the fool and serve with some shortbread biscuits.

Lemon verbena
Aloysia triphylla

Type of plant	Tender perennial
Height and spread	1.5m/1m
Best position	Sunny
Soil	Well drained
Method of propagation	Semi-ripe cuttings
Part of plant used	Leaves and flowers

Whenever I crush a leaf of lemon verbena I can close my eyes and be taken straight back to the Saturday mornings of my childhood when my sister Sue and I would each be given a weekly pack of sweets. Sue would judiciously divide them into seven small lots in order to have some every day, and I would sit and eat nearly everything all in one go, and then feel thoroughly sick. But the biggest, and my favourite, was the tube of lemon sherbert complete with liquorice dipper, which I would save until Sunday, just before bedtime. It became a ritual, rounding off the weekend with a treat. I continued the ritual – on and off – into adulthood; but now, instead of a lemon sherbert dip I occasionally have a cup of lemon verbena tea, which is very relaxing just before bed.

Lemon verbena is deciduous, so it is one of the few herbs that I preserve by drying, so I can have my tea during the winter too. You can scatter the delicate flowers over a fruit salad, or add a few to a dressing, as in the recipe below.

It is a tender plant, needing protection if the temperature falls below 4°C. For this reason I grow mine in a pot, which can be moved into an unheated greenhouse or cold frame over the dormant season. I also cover it with some horticultural fleece to be on the safe side.

LEMON VERBENA DRESSING

Recipes using lemon verbena tend to be for sweet dishes, but this dressing is just lovely with any sort of fish or shellfish. It would do equally well as a summer salad dressing, too. The orange juice adds just a hint of sweetness.

INGREDIENTS
5 tbsp olive oil
1½ tbsp lemon verbena leaves, finely chopped
1 tbsp orange juice
2 tbsp lemon juice
1 tbsp chopped chives
Salt and pepper

METHOD
- Simply put all the ingredients into a bowl and whisk together.
- Leave for 10 minutes or so before serving, to let the flavours infuse.

SUMMER MESS WITH LEMON VERBENA

This is a variation on the traditional, and very easy, recipe for Eton mess, a dessert of strawberries, cream and meringue first concocted at the famous public school. It uses the same basic ingredients, with the addition of lemon verbena. The end result is so yummy it is almost beyond description. You could use lemon balm instead of lemon verbena, but the flavour isn't as distinctive. I have also used raspberries instead of strawberries in this recipe but I really can't decide which is the most delicious ... best to make a batch of each, I think!

INGREDIENTS
500g ripe strawberries
50g caster sugar
300ml double or whipping cream
60g meringues, roughly crushed (bought ones are fine)
About 10 lemon verbena leaves, finely chopped

METHOD
- Hull and halve the strawberries and put them in a bowl, together with the sugar. Cover and leave for about an hour.
- Just before you want to serve, whip the cream to the soft peak stage and fold in the crushed meringues, strawberries and lemon verbena, reserving a little lemon verbena to use as garnish.
- Heap into sundae dishes and sprinkle each one with the reserved lemon verbena.

Lovage
Levisticum officinale

Type of plant	Hardy perennial
Height and spread	2m/1m
Best position	Full sun or partial shade
Soil	Fertile, well drained
Method of propagation	Seed, outside in the early dormant season or the early growing season; division
Part of plant used	Leaves and seeds

Lovage is a native of the mountains of the eastern Mediterranean; like many of the herbs used today, it was probably brought to our shores by the Romans.

It is best grown in full sun or partial shade in the open ground. Don't let it dry out during the growing season. Lovage is a hardy perennial, which means that it will die down over the dormant season but will come back again in the early growing season. Give it plenty of room as it can grow to a height of 2m with a spread of 1m.

The Ancient Greeks used lovage to aid digestion, and in the sixteenth century it was thought of as an aphrodisiac (a common name for it is 'love parsley'), although I can find no written record of its efficacy! Nowadays it's occasionally used to scent baths but is more commonly found in the kitchen. The flavour is strong – a combination of parsley and celery combined with a hint of aniseed – so it should be used in moderation. For those watching their salt intake, the crushed seeds can be used, sparingly, as a substitute.

LOVAGE, LETTUCE AND PEA SOUP

This soup may sound a little uninspiring, but once you've tasted it I'm sure you will agree that it's summer in a soup bowl. You may think from the recipe that adding only four or five leaves of lovage is hardly worth the effort, but it is just enough to add a piquancy without overpowering the other ingredients.

INGREDIENTS
20g butter
1 small onion, finely chopped
500ml vegetable or light chicken stock
2 little gem lettuces, finely shredded
100g peas
4 or 5 young lovage leaves, finely shredded
Salt and pepper
A few tablespoons crème fraîche, to serve

METHOD
- Melt the butter over a low heat and cook the onion until it is soft and translucent but not brown.
- Pour in the stock and bring to the boil. Reduce the heat and add the lettuce, peas and lovage leaves. Simmer gently for no more than 5 minutes.
- Season and serve in individual bowls. At the last minute, swirl some crème fraîche into the soup.

SMOKED MACKEREL PÂTÉ WITH LOVAGE

The intense flavour of smoked mackerel is a perfect foil for the equally full-bodied lovage. Both are tempered by the mild soft cheese and tanginess of the soured cream and lemon.

INGREDIENTS
2 smoked mackerel fillets, skinned and boned
120g soft cheese
1 tbsp soured cream
Juice of ½ lemon
4 or 5 young lovage leaves
Black pepper

METHOD
- Simply put all the ingredients into the bowl of a food processor, and pulse until the mixture is of the desired consistency – you can make it as coarse or smooth as you like.
- If you don't have a processor, chop the mackerel into small pieces, depending on how coarse you want your pâté to be, and chop the lovage leaves very finely. In a bowl, combine the mackerel and lovage with all the other ingredients.
- Serve with some lemon wedges and crusty bread.

Mint

Mentha spicata

Type of plant	Hardy perennial
Height and spread	45–60cm/indefinite
Best position	Sunny or light shade
Soil	Fertile, moist
Method of propagation	Softwood and root cuttings; division; layering
Part of plant used	Leaves

There are numerous species and varieties of mint – in one herb mail order catalogue I found no fewer than thirty-four! Some have hints of other flavours to them, ranging from banana to chocolate peppermint, but to my mind the best is still the common spearmint, *Mentha spicata*. This common mint is native to Mediterranean regions and was probably introduced to Britain by the Romans. In classical times mint was rubbed over tables before a banquet so that, as Pliny noted, the scent would 'stir up ... a greedy desire for meat'.

As well as spearmint, I like the slightly less pungent flavour of apple mint (*Mentha suaveolens*). The leaves are larger than spearmint and are slightly hairy – and yes, it does have an 'appley' tinge to it.

All types of mint are invasive, so grow them either in a container or in a bed of their own. Although they prefer a sunny site they will grow in light shade as long as the soil is fairly fertile and moist.

Who can imagine roast lamb without mint sauce? Although the French deride our use of mint sauce (and particularly our pared-down version) it nevertheless has a long and honourable pedigree: there is a recipe for 'Hot Mint Sauce' in the first-century volume *De Re Conquinaria* by Apicius. Mint is found in many Middle Eastern and Levantine recipes, and although it generally does not go well with many meats other than lamb, mutton or duck, it does have an affinity with various vegetables and fruit.

MINT AND PEA SHUCK SOUP

One of the things I remember about my visits to Aunty Foof was shucking peas. I know that this could only have happened during the summer months, but memory plays funny tricks on you, and I would swear now that every time I went to Aunty Foof's one of my jobs was to pick and shuck the peas. We would sit outside her back door, bowls in laps, carefully prising out the small, sweet peas from their casings – yes, the sun always shone, too! Many of the peas never made it to the cook pot because my sister and I both ate as many raw as ended up cooked.

Aunty Foof was not one to waste things, and the pea shucks were no exception. I now know that some of them were transformed into a rather potent wine – *à la* Tom and Barbara's pea pod burgundy from the TV sitcom *The Good Life*. Others found their way into a rather delicious soup. Pea and mint is a classic combination – the flavours seem to complement but not overpower one another. Rather than use fresh peas, in her version Aunty Foof used the flavour-packed shucks. Naturally she used her own mint, which had escaped the confines of its bed to run rampant through the veg patch. This never seemed to bother Aunty Foof – her reply was that at least it wasn't ground elder!

Before I share her (updated) recipe with you, let me tell you why she was called Aunty Foof, when her real name was Mary. It was because she 'foofed' things, or waited for things to 'foof' of their own accord: 'foof' was her unique catch-all term. She would 'foof' (smoke) the bees when she opened the hive; she would wait for her home-made wine to stop 'foofing' (fermenting); she waited for the bread to 'foof up' (rise) – you get the picture!

INGREDIENTS
1 tbsp oil
1 small onion, chopped
About 500g pea shucks
1ltr vegetable or chicken stock
1 tbsp double cream or crème fraîche
2 tbsp chopped mint
Salt and pepper to taste

METHOD
- Heat the oil in a large pan, and gently fry the onions until they are translucent.
- Add the pea shucks and stock, cover the pan and simmer until the shucks are cooked. (Some may never become tender because they will be too stringy.)
- Take the pan off the heat and whizz the contents in a food processor or liquidiser.
- Even at this stage the soup will be too fibrous, so you need to pass it through a sieve to end up with a nice, smooth liquid.
- Return the soup to a clean pan and stir in the cream or crème fraîche. Gently reheat without boiling.
- Just before serving, add the chopped mint.

STUFFED AUBERGINE WITH MINT

This recipe is a favourite of my daughter's, who is a vegetarian. With the addition of pine nuts and lentils to the filling it's a meal in itself. The mint and spices add another dimension to what might otherwise be a rather bland combination. Served with a green salad this recipe is enough for two people.

INGREDIENTS
1 aubergine
2 tbsp olive oil
100g puy lentils
2 tomatoes, skinned
1 medium onion, finely chopped
1 clove garlic, crushed
1 tbsp pine nuts
1 pinch ground cinnamon
1 pinch ground coriander
1 pinch ground cloves
3 tbsp mint, finely chopped

METHOD

- Preheat the oven to 200°C, gas mark 6.
- Slice the aubergine in half lengthways and score diagonal cuts in the flesh. Brush the surface with 1 tbsp of the oil and bake in the oven for about 30 minutes or until soft.
- Meanwhile, cook the lentils according to the instructions on the packet. Drain and put aside.
- Deseed and chop one of the tomatoes; slice the other one and put aside.
- Heat the remaining oil in a pan and gently cook the onions for about 5 minutes or until translucent. Add the garlic and cook for a further 5 minutes.
- Add the chopped tomatoes, lentils, pine nuts and spices and cook for a further 3 minutes.
- Scoop out the soft flesh of the cooked aubergine, being careful not to break the 'shells'. Put the flesh in the pan with the other ingredients and stir in 2 tbsp of the chopped mint.
- Fill the shells with the mixture and place the sliced tomato on the surface. Bake in the oven for 15–20 minutes, or until the filling has heated through.
- Remove the aubergine to serving plates and sprinkle with the reserved chopped mint.

GEORG'S MINT CHEESECAKE
WITH STRAWBERRIES

Whenever we go out for a meal my husband Georg always opts for cheesecake for dessert, irrespective of what he has had for main course. And it doesn't seem to matter what flavour cheesecake, either – double chocolate, blueberry, caramel, rhubarb. I came up with this recipe just for him.

INGREDIENTS
200g shortbread biscuits
150g digestive biscuits
90g unsalted butter
350g double cream
150g caster sugar
650g full-fat cream cheese
Grated zest of 1 lemon and juice of ½ lemon
A dozen or so mint leaves, finely chopped
1 punnet (about 400g) strawberries, cleaned and halved
30g sugar
2 or 3 mint leaves, finely chopped
1 dsp light, runny honey

METHOD

- Line the base of 20cm spring-form cake tin with baking parchment.
- Crush the biscuits into crumbs. I find the easiest way to do this is to put the biscuits into a stout plastic bag and then scrunch them with a rolling pin.
- Melt the butter in a pan and stir in the biscuit crumbs. Tip them into the cake tin and press them down – the idea is to have a fairly smooth surface. Pop the tin into the refrigerator for at least half an hour or until the biscuit base is firm.
- To make the filling, whisk together the cream and caster sugar until the mixture is thick. Gently fold in the cream cheese, lemon zest and mint leaves.
- Tip the filling into the cake tin, smoothing the top. Cover with film and refrigerate for three or four hours.
- Put the strawberries into a bowl and add the 30g sugar and mint. Drizzle over the honey and the juice of half a lemon and very gently fold the ingredients together so that each of the strawberries is covered with sugar, honey and lemon. Cover and leave to macerate for about half an hour.
- When you are ready to serve the cheesecake, run a palette knife around the edge and release it from the tin. Serve in slices with some strawberries on the side.

Parsley
Petroselinum crispum

Type of plant	Hardy biennial
Height and spread	30–45cm/45cm
Best position	Sunny but can cope with light shade
Soil	Good, deep, fertile – not too light
Method of propagation	Seed, outdoors in early growing season, or late growing season for dormant season use
Part of plant used	Leaves

Parsley is arguably the most well-known herb in the Western world. It is a native of central and southern Europe but is now widely grown in its various forms throughout the world. It carries with it some superstitious beliefs, one being that only a pregnant woman or a witch could grow it – well, I'm certainly not pregnant!

The most common types are the curly leaved parsley (*Petroselinum crispum*) and the flat leaved, French or Italian parsley (*Petroselinum crispum* var. *Neapolitanum*). They both require the same cultivation, namely a good, rich soil which must not be acid. They also need regular watering. Although parsley is a biennial, most people grow it as an annual because in its second year it will run to seed very quickly. If you want leaves over the dormant season, sow seed in the late growing season and protect the plants with a cloche or horticultural fleece over the dormant season.

Curly leaved parsley looks particularly attractive when grown as an edging plant in a potager. It has quite a mild flavour and is ideal as a garnish. Flat leaved parsley has a stronger flavour and is the one I tend to use in cooking.

There are few recipes where parsley appears to take centre stage, as it were; it is nearly always somewhere in the chorus, supporting the leading herb. My recipes, however, put parsley in the limelight for once.

PARSLEY SAUCE

I bet I know what you're thinking! How can she dare even contemplate including a recipe for that uninspiring gloopy, cornfloury mess which has (dis)graced many a slab of poached fish! But properly made, parsley sauce is a worthy accompaniment not only to the traditional fish and gammon, but to no end of vegetable and meat dishes.

INGREDIENTS
300ml milk
5 or 6 stems parsley, including stalks
1 small shallot, cut in half
10 black peppercorns
30g butter
15g plain flour
4 heaped tbsp chopped parsley
4 tbsp double cream
A squirtlet of lemon juice
Salt and pepper

METHOD
- Place the milk, stems of parsley, shallot and peppercorns into a pan and bring up to simmering point. Turn off the heat and allow to cool completely. This will allow the flavours to infuse.
- When the milk has cooled, strain it through a sieve to remove the parsley stems and other ingredients.
- Melt the butter in a clean pan, stir in the flour and cook, without colouring, for a few minutes. Gradually add the milk until it is all incorporated and you have a smooth, creamy sauce. I use a balloon whisk, which seems to prevent any lumps from forming.
- Simmer the sauce, stirring occasionally, for about 5 minutes or until the 'raw' taste of the flour has gone. Add the chopped parsley, cream, lemon juice and seasoning and heat through.

ORANGE AND PARSLEY SALAD

Looks – and ingredients – can be deceptive! I first came across this 'salad' when my husband's Tante (Aunt) Doris served it with cold, roasted duck breast. It was sensational, yet is simplicity itself to make.

INGREDIENTS
4 or 5 sweet oranges
A couple of handfuls of finely chopped parsley – preferably
flat leaved

METHOD
- Remove the skin and pith from the oranges and cut them into thin slices across the core, removing any pips as you go, and saving any juice.
- Layer the oranges in a shallow serving dish, sprinkling each slice with some chopped parsley; trickle any saved juice over the top.

Summer savory
Satureja hortensis

Type of plant	Half hardy annual
Height and spread	30cm/30cm
Best position	Full sun
Soil	Poor, well drained
Method of propagation	Seed, inside in the early growing season
Part of plant used	Leaves

There are two types of savory commonly used in cooking – summer savory (*Satureja hortensis*) and winter savory (*Satureja montana*). Both come from Mediterranean regions, where they grow in stony or sandy fields or along the roadside, which gives a fool-proof pointer to the sort of conditions they like.

The leaves of summer savory add a lovely peppery flavour to many summer dishes. It is widely used in continental Europe, especially in Germany where it is commonly called *Bohnenkraut* (bean herb) because it has a particular affinity with all bean dishes; and, not to put too fine a point on it, it helps alleviate flatulence. It is popular in the Balkan area too, particularly in Bulgaria where you will find *sharena sol* (colourful salt), a mixture of salt, paprika and dried summer savory, on the table instead of salt and pepper.

To reflect these two uses I have devised two recipes that have become firm favourites with family and friends.

BROAD BEAN AND FETA SALAD
WITH SUMMER SAVORY

INGREDIENTS
6 tbsp good olive oil
2 tbsp lemon juice
1 clove garlic, crushed
1 tbsp finely chopped summer savory
Salt and pepper
500g young broad beans (shelled weight)
200g feta cheese, cubed
8–10 black olives

METHOD

- In a small jug, whisk together the olive oil, lemon juice, garlic and summer savory, and season to taste.
- Bring a saucepan of water to the boil and add the broad beans.
- Return to the boil and then simmer for about 4 minutes or until the beans are just tender. Drain and refresh the beans in cold water.
- Tip the beans into a large serving bowl and coat thoroughly in the dressing.
- Add the feta cheese and olives, adjusting the seasoning as necessary.

MEATBALLS WITH SUMMER SAVORY

In Bulgaria the combination of minced pork and veal in meatballs is a common one, but if you prefer not to buy veal, then use all pork instead. Nowadays, however, you can get meat from bull calves which have been humanely raised in the UK, and this is what I use in this recipe. Look out for British-reared 'rose veal' in supermarkets. I like to serve these meatballs with some rice or pasta and a light mushroom sauce.

INGREDIENTS
300g minced pork
200g minced veal
1 small onion, very finely chopped
1 slice bread (wholemeal or white, whatever you prefer), made
into breadcrumbs
1 large egg, lightly beaten
A good pinch of salt
1 tsp paprika pepper
1 tbsp summer savory, finely chopped
2–3 tbsp plain flour
A good glug of oil for frying

METHOD
- Put all the ingredients, except the flour and oil, into a large bowl and mix thoroughly – the easiest way to do this is to get your hands in it!
- Cover and refrigerate for about an hour so that the flavours can infuse.
- Form the mixture into small balls – not too big, because you want them to cook fairly quickly – and roll each ball in flour.
- Heat the oil in a large frying pan and fry the meatballs until they are golden brown and cooked through.

Sweet cicely
Myrrhis odorata

Type of plant	Hardy perennial
Height and spread	60cm/60cm
Best position	Light shade
Soil	Humus-rich, moisture retentive, but not waterlogged
Method of propagation	Seed, outside in the early dormant season; root cuttings
Part of plant used	Leaves, flowers, seeds and root

Not too many people seem to have heard of sweet cicely but it really is a most delightful herbs. Every part of the plant is safe to eat – flowers, seeds, leaves and even the root. It's also one of the earliest plants to flower so is a boon for bees and other insects. It grows in the shade, it's a perennial, and as if all that wasn't enough, it's also a beautiful plant with fern-like leaves and frothy white flowers held on umbels. So why don't more people grow it? The answer may be its appearance, since it resembles and can easily be confused with cow parsley (*Anthriscus sylvestris*), which is harmless, or the deadly hemlock (*Conium maculatum*), which is most definitely harmful. This won't be a problem if you buy plants or seeds from a reputable source. But if in doubt, don't touch it!

If you want to grow sweet cicely from seed this is best sown in the early dormant season because the seed needs a long period of cold temperatures to germinate. If you miss the boat, all is not lost, because in the late winter or the early growing season you can mix the seeds with a little damp sand, refrigerate them for at least four weeks, and then sow them as normal.

All parts of the plant carry a sweet aniseed flavour that has been exploited for years. The leaves in particular have long been used as a sugar substitute, cutting through the tartness of rhubarb, gooseberries and plums. In savoury dishes (with chicken and prawns especially) the leaves should be added at the end of the cooking time because the flavour will be lost if cooked for too long. The young leaf tips are also good in green salads: John Gerard in his *Herbal* of 1597 described them as 'exceeding good, wholesome and pleasant among other sallad herbs'.

PRAWN AND SWEET CICELY PASTA

I was inspired by Sophie Grigson's recipe for a prawn, sweet cicely and tomato risotto to create this one using pasta. It's really easy to prepare and cook, and a winner every time. If you are using frozen prawns, make sure that they are thoroughly defrosted and dry before you begin.

INGREDIENTS
250g pasta
1 tbsp olive oil
3 shallots, finely chopped
1 clove garlic, crushed
250g fresh tomatoes, skinned, deseeded and chopped – on no account used tinned!
500g prepared prawns – raw if you can get them, but cooked will do
1 small tub crème fraîche
Salt and black pepper
3 tbsp sweet cicely, finely chopped

METHOD
- Put the pasta on to cook in plenty of boiling, salted water.
- When there is 7 minutes of cooking time left, heat the oil in a pan and sweat the shallots and garlic for 2–3 minutes over a low heat.
- Add the tomatoes and prawns and cook for a further 4 minutes. Be careful not to overcook the prawns.
- Drain the pasta and return it to the pan. Add the tomato and prawn mixture, together with the crème fraîche, salt, pepper and sweet cicely. Carefully fold everything together and transfer to a serving dish.

RHUBARB AND SWEET CICELY CRUMBLE

Here is another favourite recipe using rhubarb, the first pickings of which coincide with the emergence of sweet cicely leaves in my garden. Perhaps I should start a campaign to promote the pairing of rhubarb with sweet cicely, like gooseberries with elderflowers!

INGREDIENTS
200g plain flour
80g caster sugar
100g unsalted butter
750g rhubarb, trimmed and cut into chunks
1 tbsp honey
2 tbsp sweet cicely leaves, finely chopped

METHOD
- Preheat the oven to 180°C, gas mark 4.
- If you have a food processor, whizz the flour, sugar and butter together until you have a mixture that looks like fine breadcrumbs.
- If you don't have a processor, rub the butter into the flour until this mixture looks like fine breadcrumbs, and then add the sugar, giving it a good mix.
- Put the prepared rhubarb into an ovenproof dish, pour over the honey and sprinkle with the sweet cicely.
- Spoon the crumble mixture over the fruit base, but don't press it down, just give the dish a tap to even out the surface of the crumble.
- Bake for about 40 minutes, until the top is golden and the fruit is tender – use a skewer to test for the latter.
- Serve with custard or cream.

Sweet marjoram
Origanum majorana

Type of plant	Half hardy perennial
Height and spread	30cm/30cm
Best position	Full sun
Soil	Well drained
Method of propagation	Seed, indoors in the early growing season; softwood cuttings
Part of plant used	Leaves

So when is marjoram oregano, and vice versa? My understanding is that marjoram (or sweet marjoram) refers to *Origanum majorana* and oregano is *Origanum vulgare*. I make this distinction because *O. majorana* is less hardy than *O. vulgare* and this affects the way you grow it and use it (see the entry for oregano in the Robust Herbs section, page 146).

Sweet marjoram is, in many ways, very similar to oregano. The main difference is that sweet marjoram is not as hardy as oregano. I haven't yet been able to get it through the winter without protection, and because of this I tend to sow a new batch of seeds each year. If I remember, I take some softwood cuttings and keep them indoors over the dormant season, too. The other difference is that because sweet marjoram is less robust than oregano, it needs a shorter cooking time.

Like oregano, sweet marjoram is found in many Mediterranean dishes – sprinkle it liberally on pizza, Greek salad, fresh tomatoes ...

Crème Brûlée with Sweet Marjoram and Raspberries

Although I had come across sweet marjoram in many savoury recipes, I struggled to find any sweet ones featuring this herb. In fact, time and time again I read that the only dish that sweet marjoram doesn't work well in is a dessert. To me, this was throwing down the gauntlet, so undeterred I set about concocting a sweet recipe just to see if it could be done.

This recipe is an old-established favourite but with a twist – the cream is infused with sweet marjoram and I have included raspberries to add another layer of texture and flavour. Crème brûlée aficionados may be wincing at the mere thought of such adulteration, but I think it works quite well. This quantity makes six portions.

Ingredients
500ml double cream
1 sprig sweet marjoram, plus 6 small leaves for garnish
100g caster sugar, plus a little more for the topping
5 egg yolks
2 whole eggs
300g raspberries

- You will need six ramekin dishes.
- Preheat the oven to 160°C, gas mark 3.
- Heat the cream and sweet marjoram in a pan until just below boiling. Take off the heat and allow the marjoram to infuse for about 10 minutes.
- Meanwhile, in a bowl, whisk the sugar, egg yolks and eggs together until fluffy. Remove the marjoram from the cream and whisk the cream into the sugar and egg mixture.
- Strain the mixture through a fine sieve into a large jug.
- Divide the raspberries between the ramekin dishes, saving six for decoration. Pour the custard mixture over the fruit.
- Place the ramekins in a deep roasting tray and pour in enough hot water to come halfway up the sides of the ramekins. Bake for about 40 minutes or until the custards are just set but still a bit wobbly in the middle. Remove the ramekins from the tray and allow to cool.
- When you are ready to serve, sprinkle the top of each custard with sugar and caramelise it with a cook's blowtorch. Pop a raspberry and a leaf of marjoram on the top of each custard.

Tomato Tarts with Sweet Marjoram

I have always adored the combination of tomatoes and basil, but I tried sweet marjoram in its place in this recipe and it was every bit as good. I like to use cherry tomatoes – they can be a bit fiddly to slice, but the intense flavour is worth the effort.

Ingredients
375g puff pastry – you can buy it ready rolled
4 tbsp sun-dried tomato purée
2 tbsp marjoram, chopped
100g goat's cheese
Sliced cherry tomatoes – enough to cover the tarts
Salt and pepper
A little olive oil

Method
- Preheat the oven to 200°C, gas mark 6.
- Using a saucer or small plate, cut four circles out of the pastry and put them on a lightly oiled baking tray.
- Cut a circular groove about 2cm in from the edge of circles but do not cut all the way through. The edge will rise when the tarts are cooked but you need to leave the base intact.
- Being careful not to go beyond the groove you have cut, spread each tart with the tomato purée, sprinkle half the sweet marjoram over the puree, then crumble the cheese over the top. Place the tomato slices in a single layer over the cheese.
- Brush a little olive oil on the outer ring of pastry of each tart. Sprinkle the tarts with salt, pepper and the remaining sweet marjoram.
- Bake for 20–25 minutes, until the pastry is golden brown.

Tarragon
Artemisia dracunculus

Type of plant	Half hardy perennial
Height and spread	60cm/60cm
Best position	Warm and dry
Soil	Fertile, moist – but not waterlogged (it hates wet feet!)
Method of propagation	Softwood and root cuttings; division
Part of plant used	Leaves

There are two varieties of tarragon: French (*Artemisia dracunculus*) and Russian (*Artemisia dracunculus dracunculoides*). Do not be seduced into buying Russian tarragon, as it has an inferior flavour, verging on the unpleasant. French is by far the best, but it is difficult to cultivate, producing no viable seed and being quite tender in our non-Mediterranean climate.

It is best grown in a warm, dry position and will need protection in the dormant season, either from a layer or two of horticultural fleece or a good depth of mulch. If you grow it in a container, move it into an unheated greenhouse or cold frame for the dormant season months.

Tarragon is an essential flavouring in *sauce béarnaise* and in all French dishes described as *à l'estragon*. Tarragon is also one of the ingredients of the French *fines herbes* and has a wonderful affinity with chicken. Be warned, though – it has quite a strong flavour and a little goes a long way. It can also be used to season vinegar, and if ever I am serving a salad with chicken I always make a vinaigrette with tarragon vinegar; it's delicious.

GRILLED CHICKEN WITH TARRAGON

Chicken and tarragon is a match made in heaven and once you have tasted the sublime combination, I can almost guarantee that this will become one of your favourite recipes.

INGREDIENTS
4 chicken breasts
2 tbsp finely chopped tarragon
1 tbsp oil
Salt and black pepper

METHOD
- Take each chicken breast and carefully make a slit along the length to make a pocket. Do not cut all the way through. Push some chopped tarragon into the pockets and press the sides of the chicken together again.
- Brush each of the breasts with oil and sprinkle with salt and black pepper. Grill for about 20 minutes, turning occasionally, until the chicken is cooked through.

MUSHROOM AND TARRAGON RISOTTO

This is a pairing of flavours that I came across by accident. You may think that the tarragon would overpower the mushroom, but it works together surprisingly well, especially if you can get hold of a variety of mushrooms, rather than just the closed cup ones. The combination makes a very tasty risotto. Alternatively, fry up a handful of sliced, mixed mushrooms in a pan, throw in a few chopped tarragon leaves and serve them on some chunky, malted grain, buttered toast.

INGREDIENTS
A handful of dried porcini mushrooms
1ltr vegetable stock
2 tbsp olive oil
1 small onion, finely chopped
350g risotto rice
A glug of white wine
A knob of butter
200g mushrooms, mixed if possible, cleaned and sliced
2 tbsp crème fraîche
2 tbsp Parmesan cheese, grated
2 tbsp chopped tarragon
Salt and pepper

METHOD
- Put the dried mushrooms in a bowl, cover with warm, boiled water and leave to soak for about 20 minutes. Then drain them, reserving the soaking liquor, slice them and put them to one side. You can add the soaking liquor to the stock, but make sure you strain it thoroughly to get rid of any bits.
- Bring the stock to the boil, then keep it simmering on the hob.
- Heat 1 tbsp of the oil in a pan and gently cook the onion, without browning, until it is soft and translucent.
- Stir in the rice so that all the grains are covered in oil and cook for a couple of minutes.
- Add a glug of white wine and stir until it has evaporated.
- Then add a ladleful of stock and stir until it has been absorbed. Keep adding stock and stirring until the rice is cooked. This will take about 20 minutes.

- Meanwhile, heat the butter and remaining oil in another pan and cook the mushrooms, including the porcini.
- Take the rice off the heat and fold in the mushrooms, crème fraîche, Parmesan cheese, tarragon and seasoning.

Collections of delicate herbs

Fines herbes

You may have come across a collection of delicate herbs known as *fines herbes*. This is the classic French combination of fresh herbs: tarragon, parsley, chervil and chives. If you see it offered dried, avoid it – these herbs do not dry well. Fresh, it is a sublime combination that works well in many lightly cooked dishes; perhaps the most flavoursome is a simple omelette with finely chopped *fines herbes*, along the lines of the one that my teacher Miss Smythe-with-an-e dished up all those years ago.

I include here another recipe that uses *fines herbes*: a delicious savoury roulade. Becca, my daughter, is a vegetarian and this recipe is one of her firm favourites, so I have named it in honour of her.

Petites herbes

Unlike *fines herbes*, this collection is not a classic. In fact it is not widely known outside the Little household. As you've probably guessed, this combination is one that I have put together myself, and in keeping with tradition I have given it a French name. A bit cheeky perhaps, but I couldn't resist!

My collection consists of basil, chives, celery leaf and summer savory – a group of delicate herbs that I think work really well together. The delicate 'oniony' flavour of the chives, the warm, slightly spicy flavour of the basil, the pepperiness of summer savory, are all underpinned by the celery leaf. I have used this combination, finely chopped, sprinkled over a summer salad, in a vinaigrette, combined with cream cheese as a sandwich filling, and with main course dishes, such as the one I give here for carpaccio of beef.

Becca's Spinach Roulade with Cream Cheese and Fines Herbes

Ingredients

175g spinach, either fresh or frozen
3 eggs, separated
2 tbsp grated Parmesan cheese
150g cream cheese
1 tbsp fines herbes
1 large tomato, skinned, deseeded and chopped

Method

- Preheat the oven to 190°C, gas mark 5. Line a Swiss roll tin with non-stick baking parchment.
- Cook the spinach, if you are using fresh, then drain it and squeeze out as much moisture as you can. If you are using frozen, defrost and drain, squeezing out as much moisture as possible.
- Chop the spinach and put in a bowl. Stir in the egg yolks and Parmesan cheese.
- In a separate bowl, whisk the egg whites until they are stiff. Fold them into the spinach mixture.
- Pour the mixture into the Swiss roll tin and smooth the surface.
- Bake for about 12 minutes, until it is cooked and springy when you touch it.
- Spread a sheet of baking parchment on the work surface and turn out the cooked spinach 'cake' onto the parchment. Remove the backing paper, roll up the 'cake' and leave to cool.
- Mix the cream cheese, *fines herbes* and chopped tomato together in a bowl. Unroll the 'cake' and spread the surface with the cheese mixture. Roll up and serve.

CARPACCIO OF BEEF

If you're not keen on the idea of raw meat you may be put off by this recipe, but even my husband, who is a 'traditional Sunday roast' sort of chap, likes this! For this dish you need a really sharp knife because you have to slice the beef as thinly as you possibly can. Traditionally the beef is left completely raw, but I followed Jamie Oliver's advice and I sear the meat very briefly in very hot oil, so it has a thin crust to it.

INGREDIENTS
500g fillet of beef – don't compromise on the cut: it's expensive but you pay for the tenderness

1 tbsp oil

A handful of *petites herbes* (basil, chives, celery leaf and summer savory), finely chopped

METHOD
- Heat the oil in a pan until it is very hot. Sear the meat very briefly on all sides.
- Leave it to rest for a minute or so, and then slice it very, very thinly.
- Arrange the slices on a serving plate, and sprinkle each slice with some finely chopped herbs, pressing them in slightly so they don't all fall off when you take a slice.

What delicate herbs go with what ingredient?

If you are new to using herbs in cooking it can appear to be a bit tricky deciding which herbs go best with which ingredient. So here I start with the type of ingredient and recommend which delicate herbs would enhance the flavours even more. You can then experiment with different pairings, and find some combinations that work for you.

Meat, fish, eggs and dairy
- *Beef* – basil, chervil, parsley, summer savory, sweet marjoram, tarragon

- *Lamb* – mint, parsley, sweet marjoram
- *Pork* – chervil, parsley, summer savory
- *Chicken and turkey* – celery leaf, chervil, fennel, lemon balm, lemon thyme, parsley, summer savory, tarragon
- *Duck and goose* – celery leaf, fennel, mint, parsley, summer savory, sweet marjoram, tarragon
- *White fish* – any delicate herb goes well
- *Oily fish* – any delicate herb goes well
- *Shellfish* – chervil, dill, fennel, lemon balm, lemon thyme, parsley, sweet marjoram
- *Eggs, milk, cheese* – chervil, chives, dill, parsley, sweet marjoram, tarragon

Vegetables

- *Root vegetables* (carrots, celeriac, kohlrabi, Jerusalem artichokes, potatoes, parsnips, swede, turnips; I include leeks in this group, too) – celery leaf, chives, coriander, dill, fennel, lemon balm, lemon thyme, mint, parsley, summer savory, tarragon
- *Brassicas* (e.g. cabbage, cauliflower, broccoli, kale) – coriander, dill, fennel, lemon balm, lemon thyme, mint, parsley, sweet marjoram, tarragon
- *Legumes* (e.g. peas, beans, mange-tout) – chervil, chives, coriander, dill, fennel, lemon balm, lemon thyme, mint, parsley, summer savory, sweet marjoram, tarragon
- *Cucurbits* (e.g. cucumber, courgette, squash) – basil, chervil, chives, coriander, dill, fennel, mint, parsley, sweet marjoram

Salads

- *Leaves* – basil, celery leaf, chervil, chives, coriander, dill, fennel, lemon balm, lemon thyme, mint, parsley, summer savory, sweet cicely, sweet marjoram
- *Tomatoes* – basil, chervil, chives, dill, fennel, parsley, sweet marjoram

Desserts

The flavours of some of the delicate herbs are a good match with desserts. Particularly good are lemon balm, lemon thyme, lemon verbena, mint, sweet cicely.

Chapter 6
Robust Herbs

In this chapter we look at my collection of robust herbs. There is an entry for each herb – in alphabetical order – which gives information about what type of plant it is and how to grow it, followed by some recipes featuring the herb.

At the end of the chapter you will find some additional recipes using combinations of herbs, and a list of types of ingredients (beef, cheese, vegetables and so on) and suggestions as to which robust herb goes well with them.

Fresh versus dried

As robust herbs are available all year round, I don't see the point in using dried versions. Having said that, because these herbs contain a good amount of essential oil, they are some of the few herbs that do dry fairly successfully. It is worth bearing in mind a couple of points if you use dried: first, remember to use less dried than you would fresh, since the flavour is often more intense; second, don't keep dried herbs for too long because they will lose their pungency over a relatively short space of time.

Bay

Laurus nobilis

Type of plant	Perennial evergreen tree
Height and spread	8m/3m
Best position	Warm, sunny site, protected from cold, dry winter winds
Soil	Fertile, well drained
Method of propagation	Semi-ripe cuttings; seed sown in the early dormant season
Part of plant used	Leaves

Bay is said to have originally come from Asia Minor but it grows extensively in Mediterranean regions. The Greeks and Romans saw bay as a symbol of wisdom and glory; the laurel wreaths that were given to victorious statesmen and athletes were in fact wreaths of bay.

Bay is best grown in fertile, well-drained soil in a sheltered, sunny position. In severe dormant seasons it may need protection with a layer or two of horticultural fleece. It also makes an excellent container plant, which can be moved into an unheated greenhouse or conservatory for the dormant season.

Bay is an excellent subject for topiary (which is just as well if you use as many as I do in my cooking!), but if left to its own devices it can grow to quite a size. There was a mighty specimen of a bay tree in the village where I grew up. It grew in Old Bert's garden. (To us children he was 'Old Bert' behind his back, but 'Mr Thomas, sir' to his face.) Old Bert loved his garden, and in pride of place was his bay tree, which he himself had planted as a nipper many years before. Like most gardeners, Bert was a generous man; he quite freely allowed anyone who wanted a bay leaf for the cook pot to go into his garden and snip one off, and he supplied proper laurel wreaths for the victors at the village primary school sports day. Each Advent Sunday he would surround the trunk of his bay tree with Tilley lamps, which he would prime each night until Candlemas – it was a magical sight, especially to us children. This ritual went on for many years until the time when Old Bert fell ill and the Tilley lamps stayed in the garden shed, unlit. That spring Old Bert died, and so did the bay tree. The more superstitious in the village said that it was because somehow their spirits were intertwined. These days I am more inclined to believe that the rising heat given off by the Tilley lamps provided just enough warmth to ward off the worst of the frost. But then, sometimes, I'm not so sure …

Because the plant is evergreen, bay leaves can be picked all year round, although they can, of course, be dried. Indeed, there is much debate among cooks as to whether bay leaves should be used fresh or dried. Some say that the fresh leaves are too bitter to use straight away. I always prefer fresh, but I have found a happy medium: I pick bay leaves and then leave them in a bowl on a window sill for a couple of days before using them. These leaves seem to lose their bitterness but retain their essential flavour.

Bay usually finds its way into savoury dishes, like the first two recipes below, but it also adds an understated flavour to some sweet dishes. When my mum made a milk pudding of any description – rice pudding, or a baked custard – she always infused the milk with bay before using it. She would pop the bay leaf into a saucepan containing cold milk and then gently warm the milk to blood temperature, before removing the bay leaf and then carrying on with the recipe. I hope you like the sweet recipe using bay I have included here.

COD WITH BAY

This has to be one of the easiest dishes to prepare and cook, but don't be misled by its simplicity – even during the short cooking time, the fish will absorb some of the flavour from the bay leaves.

INGREDIENTS
4 pieces cod, about 2cm thick
2 tbsp olive oil
8 bay leaves
Salt and black pepper

METHOD
- Preheat the oven to 180°C, gas mark 4.
- Brush a heavy baking sheet with a little of the oil. Lay the pieces of fish on the sheet and top each one with two bay leaves. Brush with the remaining oil and season with salt and pepper.
- Bake until the moisture exuded from the fish starts to turn milky – about 8–10 minutes. Don't overcook the fish, otherwise it will be dry and leathery.

JANSSON'S MACKEREL TEMPTATION

The original Swedish recipe (without the bay leaves and mackerel) appears in so many cookery books that I have lost count. I've taken the liberty, however, of adding extras – the bay leaves for flavour and the mackerel to make it a meal in itself. Once you've tasted it, even with the additions, you'll know why Erik Jansson, a deeply religious man who denied himself just about everything else, succumbed to this!

INGREDIENTS
2 tins anchovy fillets in oil
2 large onions, finely sliced
1kg potatoes, peeled and cut into thin sticks
400ml double cream
Black pepper
10 bay leaves
4 mackerel fillets
Lemon wedges, to serve

METHOD
- Preheat the oven to 180°C, gas mark 4.
- Drain the anchovy fillets and heat the oil in a pan. Add the onions and cook until softened. Add the potatoes and cook until they too start to soften.
- Take off the heat and gently fold in the anchovies and cream. Season with black pepper but do not add any salt.
- Spoon half the mixture into a gratin dish, distribute the bay leaves over the surface, and spoon the rest of the potato mixture over the top. Bake for about 35 minutes, until golden brown.
- Take the dish out of the oven. Season the mackerel fillets and lay them, skin-side up, on top of the potatoes. Return the dish to the oven and bake for a further 6–10 minutes, depending on the thickness of the fillets, until the mackerel is just cooked. Serve with some lemon wedges.

QUINCE COMPOTE WITH BAY

I love quince. Toady, my bee-keeping friend, has a tree in his garden and every autumn I am treated to a basketful of those lovely, pear-shaped fruits. They are best eaten cooked and this simple recipe is ideal. You can eat them cooked just as they are, or you can strain off the cooking liquor then slice or purée them to use as a fruit base in a tart. If you can't get hold of quinces, hard pears will do just as well.

INGREDIENTS
150ml white wine
200ml water
100g honey (or half honey, half sugar)
2 quinces
2 cloves
3 bay leaves

METHOD
- Pour the wine and water in a saucepan and add the honey (or honey and sugar). Heat gently, stirring occasionally, until the honey has dissolved.
- Meanwhile, peel, quarter and core the quinces. Be careful – the quince will be as hard as a rock and are therefore devilishly hard to prepare. Pop each quarter into the saucepan as you prepare it to prevent it from discolouring.
- Increase the heat to a simmer and add the cloves and bay leaves.
- Cook for about 40 minutes or longer until the fruit is tender.
- Allow to cool. The fruit, together with its cooking liquor, will keep for up to a week in the refrigerator.

Celery leaf

See the Delicate Herb section, page 68.

Chervil

See the Delicate Herb section, page 71.

Garlic

Allium sativum

Type of plant	Hardy perennial bulb, grown as an annual
Height and spread	20cm/30cm
Best position	Sunny, warm site
Soil	Fertile, well drained
Method of propagation	Individual cloves, outside in early to mid dormant season
Part of plant used	Bulbs, stems (known as scapes)

In a moment of recklessness I watched a *Carry On* film (no comments, please) in which Henry VIII (you've guessed it, Sid James) eagerly meets his future French wife, Queen Marie (the incomparable Joan Sims). His rampant ardour, however, is soon utterly deflated because she reeks of garlic. If you follow Queen Marie's example and munch on raw cloves, you too can repel any unwanted advances in a matter of seconds. Cooked garlic, though, exudes a subtle flavour, and adds a discreet layer which permeates the other ingredients in a dish.

There are many varieties of British-grown garlic available these days; my favourites are 'Early Purple Wight' and 'Lautrec Wight'. The latter is what is known as a hard-neck garlic, which means that it produces a flowering stalk – the scape. This can be snapped off and cooked – in fact, it is best to remove it because you will get a much bigger bulb of garlic if you do.

You can add garlic to so many dishes that it would probably need a whole cookery book to do it justice, but here are a couple of my favourite recipes.

Chicken with 40 cloves of garlic

'Ali chicken', as my children used to call it – because of the 40 cloves, and after the beloved folk tale about Ali Baba and the 40 thieves. Don't be put off by the amount of garlic. When it's cooked it becomes soft and creamy – the perfect accompaniment to the chicken.

Ingredients
4–6 bulbs garlic – enough to yield the 40 or so cloves required
1 chicken – free range or organic
100ml olive oil
½ lemon
300ml white wine or water

Method
- Preheat the oven to 180°C, gas mark 4.
- Divide the bulbs of garlic into cloves; discard the papery bits, but do not peel the individual cloves.
- Some people like to brown the chicken before it goes into the pot, but I just smear it with some of the oil. Tuck the half lemon in the cavity of the chicken and put the chicken in an ovenproof dish with a tight-fitting lid.
- Arrange the garlic around the chicken and then add the rest of the oil and the wine or water. Cover and bake in the oven for 1½ hours or until the chicken is very tender.
- Remove the chicken from the dish, and discard the lemon. Scoop out the cloves of garlic from the liquor and serve them with the chicken: you can squish out the soft garlic as you eat the chicken.

PASTA WITH SCAPES

This recipe makes the most of scapes and any other fresh green vegetable that is available on the day. I love it with fresh peas or mange-tout and rocket, but experiment and find your favourite combination.

INGREDIENTS
250g wholewheat pasta – penne or similar
1 tbsp olive oil
A handful of scapes, cut into 3cm pieces
A handful of fresh peas or mange-tout
A handful of young rocket leaves
1 small tub crème fraîche
Salt and black pepper
Parmesan cheese shavings for garnish

METHOD
- Cook the pasta according to manufacturer's instructions; it needs to be drained and ready to use when the vegetables have finished cooking.
- Heat the oil in a large saucepan and sweat the scapes for 2–3 minutes over a low heat.
- Add the peas or mange-tout, cover the pan and cook for 5 minutes.
- Stir in the rocket, crème fraîche, and salt and pepper.
- Combine the vegetable mixture with the cooked pasta, sprinkle with Parmesan shavings and serve.

Horseradish

Armoracia rusticana

Type of plant	Hardy perennial
Height and spread	1m/30cm
Best position	Sunny, but will tolerate dappled shade
Soil	All but very dry
Method of propagation	Root cuttings
Part of plant used	Root

My first memory of horseradish is in the ubiquitous sauce served with roast beef. I must have been fairly young at the time because I was enduring (yes, that is what it was!) one of my gran's 'Sunday Lunches'. Me, my sister and my cousin (who I didn't like very much) were sat politely, being seen but not heard, kicking one another under the table, eating our lunch. Suddenly something hit the back of my throat and I spat out the entire contents of my mouth all over my roast beef dinner – and over some of my cousin's. You can imagine the consequences – no more lunch (or tea), sent to sit on the stool in the kitchen in disgrace until being taken home and put to bed. Unbeknown to me, my dear cousin had dolloped a spoonful of horseradish sauce on my Yorkshire pud. He never owned up, of course, and to add insult to injury, I found out later that he had been given my serving of jelly and ice cream as a reward for being so well behaved. Creep.

It's taken years to get over that emotional and condimental scar. Only now can I appreciate the pungent, powerful flavour of horseradish, and below I give you my recipe for horseradish sauce. It's good with roast beef and smoked mackerel – the traditional dishes to serve it with – but I also like it with fatty poultry like duck or goose. Interestingly, once cooked, its heat and spiciness is tempered and it adds an almost delicate flavour to dishes.

A word of warning: when you are preparing and grating the horseradish there is no way to avoid tears running down your face as if you are watching a film of the most heart-rending love story of all time. I've tried grating it outside in the open air, squinting, wearing swimming goggles ... In fact, the only foolproof way to avoid the volatile oil is to get some other fool to grate it for you!

In these recipes you can use either fresh horseradish, or horseradish that has been grated when it was harvested and kept in vinegar – either way there will be sufficient oompf!

Strictly speaking, horseradish is more of a vegetable than a herb, but because of the way it is used (in small quantities), I think it is best put into the herb category. Because of the way it grows, it really needs a bed of its own, or better still, plant it in a dustbin or other deep container. Growing it like this means that it will be much easier to harvest the root, and will keep the plant in bounds – even a small amount of root left in the ground will form a new plant.

VEGETABLE AND HORSERADISH GRATIN

INGREDIENTS
A knob of butter
3 tbsp grated horseradish
400ml double cream
Salt and pepper
5 medium potatoes, peeled
About 300g celeriac, peeled
2 parsnips, peeled
5 tbsp grated cheese – Parmesan, Cheddar, whatever takes your fancy

METHOD
- Preheat the oven to 160°C, gas mark 3.
- Grease an ovenproof dish with a little butter. In a bowl, mix together the horseradish, cream and some seasoning.
- Slice the vegetables into even thicknesses – about 0.5cm. Layer them in the dish, and pour over the cream mix. Scatter the cheese over the top and bake for 1–1½ hours, or until the top is golden and the vegetables tender.

HORSERADISH SAUCE

As well as the fiery horseradish, this sauce contains some pink peppercorns, which aren't actually peppercorns at all but they do give a peppery hit to the sauce. They also add a delicate, rosy hue – to lull everyone into a false sense of security. (Perhaps it's my subconscious trying to pay back my cousin for his prank all those years ago – or perhaps it's just that I have a rather wicked side!)

INGREDIENTS
100ml crème fraîche
100ml thick yoghurt
Squeeze of lemon juice
1 tbsp grated horseradish
1 scant tsp pink peppercorns

METHOD
- Simply fold all the ingredients together in a bowl – that's it!

Hyssop
Hyssopus officinalis

Type of plant	Hardy, semi-evergreen perennial
Height and spread	45cm/30cm
Best position	Sunny
Soil	Well drained
Method of propagation	Seed, inside in the early growing season; softwood cuttings
Part of plant used	Leaves and flowers

Hyssop is native to southern Europe, the Near East and southern Russia. Its use goes back to antiquity when it is recorded as being more of a medicinal or purifying herb than a culinary one. Hyssop could always be found in monastery gardens, as it was known as a 'cure-all' for diverse complaints from acne to worms. Indeed John Gerard, in his *Herbal* of 1597, left hyssop 'altogether without description, as being a plant so well knowne that it needeth none'. The same is not true today since it figures only rarely in modern recipes.

Hyssop is a sun-worshipper and must have well-drained soil. It makes an ideal low hedge: trim back the flowers in the early dormant season, and in the early growing season give the plants a 'haircut' to keep them in shape. It also makes a perfect container plant.

To my mind, hyssop is an underrated culinary herb and deserves to be used more often. Both leaves and flowers have a warm, spicy flavour, suggestive of a mixture of thyme, rosemary and mint. It combines well with fatty meats like pork, lamb, goose or duck. Surprisingly it also works with fruit, particularly plums and peaches. It has quite a strong flavour, however, so use sparingly.

DUCK BREAST WITH HYSSOP

INGREDIENTS
1 duck breast per person
For each duck breast you will need:
Leaves from 1 sprig hyssop
1 dsp thick honey
1 clove garlic, crushed
Salt and pepper
75ml water

METHOD
- Preheat the oven to 200°C, gas mark 6.
- Make an incision in each duck breast to form a pocket – do not slice all the way through.
- Mix the hyssop, half the honey, garlic, and some salt and pepper together in a bowl. Open the pocket in the duck breast and smear the inside cavity with the mixture. Press the sides together.
- Place the duck breasts in an oven-proof dish and pour in the water.
- Bake for about 25 minutes or until they are cooked through. Take out of the dish, cover and set aside.
- Pour the juices from the dish into a saucepan and simmer over a medium heat until reduced by half. Stir in the remaining honey and serve with the duck.

PLUMS WITH HYSSOP

I first came across the use of hyssop in a fruit recipe in Sophie Grigson's book on herbs: she uses it with peaches. I thought it might work with some seasonal British fruit, such as plums, which I'm glad to say it does.

INGREDIENTS
About 3 or 4 ripe plums per person, halved and stoned
30g sugar
1 sprig hyssop
Juice of ½ lemon

METHOD
- Put the plums in a bowl with the hyssop. Sprinkle with sugar and pour over the lemon juice. Stir carefully and set aside to macerate for half an hour.
- Transfer the entire contents of the bowl to a pan and cook very gently for a few minutes until the plums are just tender.
- Discard the hyssop. Put the plums and the juice into a serving bowl and allow to cool.
- Serve the plums on their own or with cream or crème fraîche, and a shortbread biscuit.

Lavender
Lavandula sp.

Type of plant	Hardy evergreen shrub
Height and spread	45–60cm/30–60cm
Best position	Sunny
Soil	Well drained
Method of propagation	Seed, inside in the early growing season; semi-ripe cuttings
Part of plant used	Flowers

Lavender is native to dry, rocky regions of the Mediterranean. Its name comes from the Latin word *lavare* meaning 'to wash', and the Romans used lavender to scent their bathwater. It is thought that it was indeed the Romans who brought lavender to our shores, although no reference to it has been found before 1265, when it is recorded in a manuscript of that date. There are many species of lavender: the hardiest are *Lavandula angustifolia* and *Lavandula* x *intermedia*, which can withstand temperatures down to minus 10°C and more, provided they are not exposed to cold winds and don't have wet feet.

For my money the best lavender is one of the varieties of *Lavandula angustifolia*. I particularly like 'Hidcote' because it has beautiful dark flowers, makes a shapely bush, and has a sweeter fragrance than many other varieties. If you want a slightly shorter variety, try *L. angustifolia* 'Peter Pan'.

Lavender has long been used in medicine for a range of ailments, from insomnia to fungal infections. It was used widely as a strewing herb to deter insects, and it is a constituent, of course, of many perfumes.

Ask a creative person what they might do with lavender flowers and they would probably suggest drying them to put in lavender bags to scent their clothes or household linen. However, lavender flowers have long been used in cooking, in both sweet and savoury dishes. Lavender fell out of favour for quite some years, but I am pleased to see that it is making a comeback, particularly in sweet dishes. Don't ignore it in savoury recipes, though – it adds a piquancy that is unsurpassed.

LAVENDER STUFFING

Here is a recipe that goes well with chicken and is especially tasty when used in a rolled shoulder of lamb. In southern France, and particularly in Provence, lambs are grazed in pasture where lavender grows wild; this helps to develop a unique flavour in the meat.

INGREDIENTS
50g wholemeal breadcrumbs
1 large free-range egg
1 onion, finely chopped
1 tsp lavender flowers, stripped from the flower spike and chopped
Leaves from a sprig of rosemary, chopped

METHOD
- Combine all the ingredients. Use to stuff a chicken, or a rolled shoulder of lamb.
- Or bake separately for about 20 minutes at 180°C, gas mark 4, until browned.

THE BEE-KEEPER'S
AND HERB GROWER'S TART

That is, caramelised onion, goat's cheese and lavender tart. I first came across the combination of caramelised onion and goat's cheese when I had lunch with Toady, my bee-keeping mate. He suggested that honey would give even more depth of flavour to the onion, and I thought that a smidgeon of lavender added to the goat's cheese would contrast well. I tried it, and have to say that Toady was right about the honey.

INGREDIENTS
4 large onions, thinly sliced
A glug of oil
1 tbsp honey
375g shortcrust pastry
200g goat's cheese
1 tbsp lavender flowers, roughly chopped
Salt and black pepper

METHOD
- You will need four individual flan or quiche tins.
- First, caramelise the onions. Heat the oil in a pan and gently fry the onions, stirring occasionally, until they start to turn golden brown.
- Add half the honey to pan and continue frying. Keep an eye on the onions; you don't want them to burn, but don't stir too often otherwise they will not caramelise.
- Continue cooking the onions until they get to the point where they are brown and very soft and there is no moisture left in the pan. This can take anything from 40 minutes to an hour, depending on the onions and your cooker! At this point, add the rest of the honey and heat through. Take off the heat and set aside.
- Preheat the oven to 200°C, gas mark 6.
- Roll out the pastry and line the flan or quiche tins.
- Carefully spread the onions over the bottom of the pastry.
- In a bowl, mix together the goat's cheese and lavender flowers. Cover the onions with the cheese. Bake for 20–25 minutes, until the pastry is golden brown, then serve with a green, herby salad.

LAVENDER BISCUITS

I first tasted lavender biscuits in a tea shop while on holiday in Derbyshire – this was when I was living in Sussex and anything north of Watford Gap was almost *terra incognita*! I don't remember much about the rest of the holiday but the subtle taste of those biscuits has stayed with me for more than 30 years. Here's my version of them. The recipe makes about 15 biscuits.

INGREDIENTS
100g butter
50g caster sugar
175g self-raising flour
1 tsp lavender flowers, stripped from the flower spike

METHOD
- Preheat the oven to 150°C, gas mark 2.
- Cream the butter and sugar together until light.
- Add the flour and lavender flowers to the mixture and lightly knead until it forms a dough.
- Carefully roll out the dough on a lightly floured board to about 3mm thick. Cut out rounds using a 7.5cm cutter.
- Arrange the biscuits on a lightly greased baking sheet and bake for about 30 minutes, or until the biscuits are a pale golden brown colour.
- Cool on a wire rack and store in an airtight container – if they don't all get eaten straight away!

Myrtle

Myrtus communis

Type of plant	Hardy, evergreen perennial
Height and spread	1m/1m
Best position	Full sun
Soil	Fertile, well drained
Method of propagation	Softwood cuttings
Part of plant used	Leaves, berries

I have to admit, I am a bit of a myrtle virgin. Although I have had myrtle growing in my garden for a number of years, it is only fairly recently that I have started using it in my cooking. I use the leaves mostly as I would bay, but not so many of them because the flavour is spicier than bay and slightly bitter. And I sometimes use the berries in place of juniper berries in dishes that feature strongly flavoured meat such as venison, mutton or pheasant.

In Sardinia the leaves and berries are used to make a liqueur called Mirto, which apparently has quite a kick to it. Also in Sardinia, myrtle is often married with pork so I have experimented with my favourite way with belly pork and come up with the recipe below. And I wondered if myrtle might be a little too pungent to use in a sweet recipe, but I added some leaves to my 'foraged fruit' jam and it worked rather well.

Myrtle requires the same sort of growing conditions as bay. Although it's a Mediterranean plant, it's pretty hardy, but will struggle if the ground is too moist. If you live in an area prone to cold winters, plant it in a pot which can be put in a frost-free place.

BELLY PORK WITH MYRTLE

INGREDIENTS
A piece of boned pork belly, about 1kg in weight, rind left on
2 tsp sunflower oil
1 tbsp apple juice
2–3 tbsp runny honey
2 cloves garlic, crushed
6 myrtle leaves, slightly bruised

METHOD
- Score the rind of the pork.
- Combine the oil, apple juice, 2 tbsp honey, garlic and myrtle leaves
  together in a dish. Put the pork in the dish, rind-side up, and
  spread it with the marinade. Cover and leave for up to four hours.
- Preheat the oven to 180°C, gas mark 4.
- Remove the pork from the dish (don't throw the marinade away)
  and lay on a rack in a roasting tin, rind-side up. Cook for about an
  hour and then baste with some of the reserved marinade.
- Cook for another 1½ hours or so, basting occasionally with the
  juices from the pork and more marinade if necessary.
- Brush the remaining tablespoon of honey over the rind and
  continue cooking for a further 30 minutes without basting, so that
  the honey caramelises and forms a glaze.
- Remove from the oven and allow the pork to rest for 15 minutes
  before you serve it.

FORAGED FRUIT JAM WITH MYRTLE

My favourite combination of foraged fruit jam is blackberries from a farm hedgerow, bilberries from heathland up on the Lancashire fells, and some apples from my neighbour's garden. Naturally, I have everyone's permission to gather the fruit and I always give them a jar or two of the jam as repayment come Christmas.

INGREDIENTS
1kg fruit – I use a more or less equal mixture of blackberries,
bilberries and cooking apples
500ml water
Juice of 1 large lemon
About 10 myrtle leaves
1kg granulated sugar
150g runny honey

METHOD
- Prepare the fruit by peeling, coring and slicing the apples, discarding any bruised fruit, and picking over the blackberries and bilberries to remove any leaves, etc.
- Tie the myrtle leaves together in a piece of muslin.
- Put the fruit into a preserving pan with the water, lemon juice and muslin bag of leaves. Put the pan on the hob and heat very gently until the mixture warms through.
- Add the sugar and stir gently until it has all dissolved. Then add the honey and increase the heat to bring the mixture to boiling point.
- Boil rapidly for about 5 minutes. Test for setting point using a thermometer.
- Remove from the heat, take out the muslin bag, and stir very gently if the surface is a little scummy.
- Pour into sterilised jars and seal.

Oregano
Origanum vulgare

Type of plant	Hardy perennial
Height and spread	30cm/30cm
Best position	Full sun
Soil	Well drained
Method of propagation	Softwood cuttings; seed in the early growing season; division
Part of plant used	Leaves

There always seems to be confusion between oregano and marjoram, the common names apparently being interchangeable. The Latin genus name is the same for both: namely, *Origanum*.

Personally, I use the name marjoram for the herb known as sweet marjoram, whose Latin name is *Origanum majorana*, and oregano for the other type I use in cooking, namely *O. vulgare*. I tend to make this distinction because *O. majorana* is less hardy (it won't cope with temperatures below freezing) and I grow it as an annual (see sweet marjoram in the Delicate Herb section, page 113), whereas *O. vulgare* is hardy (down to minus 15°C) and I grow it as a perennial.

I wouldn't be without oregano or marjoram growing in my garden, not only because they enhance so many recipes, but because if you leave some to flower they attract so many bees. The nectar has a very high sugar content – up to 80 per cent. The bees love it so much that I swear you can see them circling in a holding formation above the flowers, like aeroplanes waiting for a landing slot!

All species of *Origanum* appear to originate from the Mediterranean, but nowadays many can be found growing wild in various places, including the chalk downs of southern Britain. In addition there are a number of decorative forms of oregano with different coloured leaves or flowers – all can be used in cooking, but to my mind the straightforward *Origanum vulgare* has the best flavour.

Oregano is used extensively in Greek and Italian cooking and it is the main herb of the Neapolitan pizza. If the recipe calls for a longer cooking time, make sure you use oregano rather than sweet marjoram – it is more robust.

JAMES'S SHEPHERD'S PIE MEAT SAUCE

I use a Mediterranean-inspired meat sauce for my shepherd's pie. The addition of a fair amount of oregano to this lamb-based sauce (not beef, which would make it cottage pie) lifts it to another level, and I also add some tomatoes. You can also use the sauce for pasta, or in moussaka. My son James loves this versatile sauce so much that I have named it after him.

INGREDIENTS
1 tbsp oil
1 large onion, chopped
450g minced lamb
1 tbsp flour
100ml stock
2 ripe tomatoes, skinned, deseeded and chopped
1 generous tbsp tomato purée
Salt and pepper
1 tbsp chopped, fresh oregano (or 1 tsp dried)

METHOD
- Heat the oil in a pan and fry the onions until they are soft and golden. Take them out of the pan and leave to one side.
- In the same pan, brown the mince, then return the onions to the pan. Stir in the flour and cook for a couple of minutes. Gradually add the stock and then the tomatoes, tomato purée, salt, pepper and oregano.
- Simmer gently for about 10 minutes, stirring occasionally to prevent the sauce from catching.
- If you are making shepherd's pie, prepare the potato topping while the sauce is cooking.

GOAT'S CHEESE STACK WITH OREGANO

This is a really simple recipe in which the different ingredients just seem to work so well together. You could use sweet marjoram instead of oregano, but I think the slightly stronger flavour of oregano is better.

INGREDIENTS
1 tbsp oregano, finely chopped – reserve a little for garnish
3–4 tbsp olive oil
Salt and pepper
2 round goat's cheeses – the semi-soft kind with a bloomy, white rind – sliced into two so that you have four 'rounds'
4 thick slices ciabatta bread
1 small aubergine, cut into 8 slices of about 1cm – adjust the thickness as necessary
2 large beefsteak tomatoes, each cut into 4 slices

METHOD
- Combine the oregano, oil, salt and pepper together in a shallow dish, big enough to take the rounds of cheese in a single layer. Marinate the cheese in the oil mixture for about an hour, turning occasionally.
- Preheat a non-stick griddle pan. Toast the ciabatta in the griddle pan on both sides and put on a serving plate.
- Take the rounds of goat's cheese out of the marinade and put them to one side.
- Dip the slices of aubergine in the marinade, then cook them in the griddle pan, turning occasionally until they are golden. Put to one side.
- Cook the cheese in the griddle pan quickly on both sides, until it is just beginning to melt.
- Now assemble the 'stack'. Place a slice of aubergine on the ciabatta, then a slice of tomato, a slice of cheese, another slice of tomato, and finally a slice of aubergine. Sprinkle with the reserved oregano and serve immediately with some rocket on the side.

CARROT, CELERIAC AND OREGANO SALAD

This simple salad is just the thing during late winter and early spring when your taste buds tell you that they want something fresh, rather than steaming stews and comforting casseroles.

INGREDIENTS

225g carrots, grated
225g celeriac, grated
1 tbsp olive oil
1 tbsp runny honey
Juice and zest of ½ lemon
1 tbsp oregano, chopped
Salt and pepper

METHOD

- Put the grated carrots and celeriac in a bowl. In a separate bowl, mix together the oil, honey, lemon juice and zest, oregano, salt and pepper.
- Pour the dressing over the carrots and celeriac and gently stir in.
- Leave for an hour and stir again before serving.

Parsley

See the Delicate Herbs section, page 104.

Rosemary
Rosmarinus officinalis

Type of plant	Hardy evergreen shrub
Height and spread	90cm/60cm
Best position	Sunny, with shelter from cold winds
Soil	Well drained
Method of propagation	Seed, indoors in the early growing season; semi-ripe cuttings; layering
Part of plant used	Leaves

Rosemary is native to scrubby, coastal regions of the Mediterranean – its Latin name, *Rosmarinus*, means 'dew of the sea'. It also grows abundantly inland: the French gardener Olivier de Serres noted in the sixteenth century that in Provence rosemary was so abundant that its woody stems were used as fuel in bread ovens. Rosemary is a symbol of fidelity and remembrance; as Sir Thomas More (1478–1535) wrote: 'As for Rosemarine, I let it run all over my garden walls, not only because my bees love it, but because 'tis the herb sacred to remembrance, and, therefore, to friendship.'

Being a Mediterranean herb, rosemary enjoys a warm, sunny position. Although it's hardy and can withstand temperatures down to minus 10°C and more in a sheltered position, the one thing it really hates is wet feet. Give it well-drained, verging on poor, soil.

While browsing a mail order herb catalogue I was surprised to see more than twenty types of rosemary listed. As well as the straightforward *Rosmarinus officinalis*, others have diverse and colourful-sounding names, such as *R. officinalis* 'Miss Jessop's Upright' (which always brings to mind primary school, sitting very straight in my chair, arms folded, barely daring to breathe, let alone speak), and *R. officinalis* 'Majorca Pink' (I can't help but hope that the flowers are a vivid, candy-floss pink – quite the floozie compared to Miss Jessop!).

Rosemary is usually paired with lamb or chicken, but it goes well with, as you would expect, anything remotely Mediterranean. Don't just use it in savoury dishes, though; experiment a little with some sweet ones, like my recipe for chocolate ganache, below.

RACK OF LAMB WITH ROSEMARY

The pairing of lamb with rosemary is a classic one, and no wonder – the combination is sublime. This recipe has only one addition – garlic – so that the flavour of the lamb and rosemary shines through.

INGREDIENTS
An 8-bone rack of lamb, trimmed
A glug of olive oil
2 tbsp chopped rosemary
3 cloves garlic, crushed

METHOD
- Mix the oil, rosemary and garlic together and rub it all over the lamb. Cover it and refrigerate for an hour.
- Take the lamb out of the fridge and preheat the oven to 190°C, gas mark 5. Place the lamb in a roasting tin and cook for 30–40 minutes, or until it is cooked to your liking: for pink meat, 25–30 minutes is probably enough; if you like it well done, allow 40–45 minutes.
- Remove from the oven and allow the lamb to rest for 8–10 minutes before carving – allow two bones per person.

RED CABBAGE WITH ROSEMARY

If you have been put off red cabbage in the past, either because it has been boiled or braised to within an inch of its life and become a dull, grey-coloured mush, or because it has been pickled and the jar has been sitting on the larder shelf since Boxing Day, take heart! This recipe, I hope, will change your mind about this most underrated vegetable.

It goes well with just about any meat dish – I serve it with Lancashire hotpot, something my dyed-in-the-wool Lancastrian friends positively wince at!

INGREDIENTS
2 tbsp olive oil

1 red cabbage, trimmed and cut into quarters through the stem

Salt

A pinch of sugar

250ml red wine

125ml vegetable or chicken stock

3 sprigs rosemary

METHOD
- Heat the oil in a saucepan or flameproof casserole dish big enough to accommodate the cabbage comfortably. Add the cabbage quarters and brown them lightly on all sides – do not let them burn.
- Add the salt, sugar, red wine and stock and bring to the boil. Then reduce the heat to a simmer and add the rosemary.
- Turn the cabbage occasionally so that it is cooked evenly. When the cabbage is just tender – this should take about 10 minutes – take it out of the pan and keep warm. Don't overcook – err on the side of crispness rather than mush!
- Turn up the heat and reduce the liquid in the pan to about 3 tbsp. Discard the rosemary and serve the liquor with the cabbage.

CHOCOLATE ROSEMARY GANACHE

Everyone, almost without exception, loves chocolate. But how many have tried chocolate with rosemary? It may seem an odd combination, I grant you, but it really does work: the subtle flavour of rosemary permeates the chocolate without overpowering it. I use this ganache as a cake filling and it's interesting to see my friends debating what sort of chocolate I have used – disbelief turns to amazement when I tell them that it is rosemary that gives that touch of *je ne sais quoi*!

You can also make the ganache into chocolates, by shaping it into balls, coating them in cocoa powder and popping them into individual sweetie cases: they make a lovely present. This recipe is enough for a generous cake filling.

INGREDIENTS
250g good-quality chocolate, minimum 70 per cent cocoa solids
250ml double or whipping cream
A sprig of rosemary

METHOD
- Pour the cream into a small saucepan, add the sprig of rosemary, and bring it to the boil.
- Meanwhile, break the chocolate into small pieces and put into a bowl.
- Remove the cream from the heat and gradually strain it through a sieve over the chocolate, stirring all the time so that the milk and chocolate are completely amalgamated into a smooth mixture.
- Allow to cool, and then use as desired.

Sage
Salvia officinalis

Type of plant	Hardy evergreen perennial
Height and spread	30–60cm/45cm
Best position	Warm and sunny
Soil	Well drained, not acid
Method of propagation	Semi-ripe cuttings; seed, inside in the early growing season; layering
Part of plant used	Leaves

Sage has always been a highly prized herb, not only in the kitchen but also as a medicine. Its name is testament to this: the genus name, *Salvia*, is said to be derived from the Latin *salvere*, meaning to save or heal, while the species name, *officinalis*, comes from the Latin *opificina*, meaning a herb store or pharmacy. An Arabic proverb claims: 'He who has sage in his garden will not die.'

Salvia officinalis, known as common, garden or broad-leaved sage, is the best-known variety for culinary use, and has pale grey-green, velvety leaves. Other varieties, notably gold sage (*Salvia officinalis* 'Icterina') and purple sage (*Salvia officinalis* Purpurascens Group), which have colourful leaves, are just as good in the kitchen, although their flavour might not be as strongly aromatic as common sage. Sage requires a sunny position with well-drained soil. Although it is a Mediterranean plant, it will survive British winters without protection, as long as its feet aren't wet!

Sage has a wonderful affinity with pork, and what would our poultry do without sage and onion stuffing? As with many other herbs, though, it's worth breaking the bonds a little and experimenting with new ways of using old favourites – which is what I have done with the apple and sage cake, below. First, though, a tried and tested combination.

SAGE-ENCRUSTED PORK

This recipe is very straightforward, but delicious for all that. The breadcrumb coating works equally well with a tenderloin of pork, coated, cooked whole and then sliced.

INGREDIENTS
4 pork loin chops
Breadcrumbs made from 4 slices of a fresh wholemeal loaf
4 tbsp chopped fresh sage
Salt and black pepper
2 tbsp Dijon mustard (English mustard is too fiery)

METHOD
- Preheat the oven to 180°C, gas mark 4.
- Dry the chops thoroughly with kitchen paper.
- Mix the breadcrumbs, chopped sage, salt and pepper together and spread out on a large plate.
- Spread each side of the chops with a thin layer of mustard.
- Then thoroughly coat each chop with the breadcrumb mixture, pressing it in firmly.
- Place the chops on a rack over a roasting tin and cook in the oven for about 25 minutes, or until cooked through.

UPSIDE-DOWN APPLE AND SAGE CAKE

INGREDIENTS

2 eating apples – I like Cox's but use your favourite
1 large Bramley apple
Juice of 1 lemon
200g butter
200g soft brown sugar
3 large eggs, lightly beaten
200g self-raising flour
1 tbsp finely chopped sage leaves
1 tbsp demerara sugar

METHOD

- Line a 20cm cake tin or 2lb loaf tin with non-stick baking parchment (the ready-formed ones save a lot of time).
- Preheat the oven to 180°C, gas mark 4.
- Peel and core the apples. Thinly slice the eating apples and cut the Bramley into small cubes. Put them all into a bowl containing the lemon juice to prevent them from discolouring.
- In a mixing bowl, cream the butter and soft brown sugar together until they are fluffy. Gradually beat in the eggs, a little at a time.
- Sift the flour into the bowl and add the chopped sage. Gently fold the dry ingredients into the mixture.
- Sprinkle the demerara sugar over the bottom of the cake tin. Drain the apple and arrange the sliced eating apple decoratively on top of the sugar, then put the cubed Bramley apple on top of this. Spoon the cake mixture over the apples.
- Bake for about 1 hour, until golden. The cake will be ready when a skewer inserted into the centre of the cake comes out clean. If the cake is looking a little too brown, cover it with a sheet of brown paper for the last 15 minutes or so.
- Remove from the oven and allow to cool for about 20 minutes before taking it out of the tin. Serve with clotted cream – yum.

Thyme

Thymus sp.

Type of plant	Hardy, evergreen perennial
Height and spread	30cm/30cm
Best position	Warm and sunny, sheltered
Soil	Well drained
Method of propagation	Seed, indoors in the early growing season; semi-ripe cuttings; layering; division
Part of plant used	Leaves

According to the Royal Horticultural Society, there are about 350 species of thyme (including three that grow wild in Britain). The three most widely used in the kitchen are garden or common thyme (*Thymus vulgaris*), lemon thyme (*Thymus citriodorus*) and broad-leaved thyme (*Thymus pulegioides*). They are native to rocky sites and dry, usually chalky, grasslands of Europe, western Asia and North Africa. This gives us a good idea about how to grow them: they like a warm, sunny site with well-drained soil and they hate wet feet, particularly during the dormant season.

Thyme is indispensable in the kitchen. One of its great advantages is that it can withstand long, slow cooking (hence it is one of my 'robust squad'), and teamed up with wine, onion and garlic it forms the basis of many famous dishes: *boeuf bourguignon*, *navarin* of lamb and *coq au vin*, to name just three. Thyme is also one of the main ingredients of the classic *bouquet garni* and *herbes de Provence* (see pages 163 and 166). Lemon thyme adds a subtle hint of citrus in fish and chicken dishes, and you can also use it in desserts.

LANCASHIRE HOTPOT WITH THYME

Although not born and bred in Lancashire, I certainly feel at home here and have made some tremendous friends. Here is a recipe for hotpot from one of them – I don't know how authentic it is, but I do know that it tastes delicious!

I usually seal meat before I put it in a stew or casserole but my friend doesn't bother, and I have to say it doesn't seem to make any difference to the end result.

INGREDIENTS
1kg shoulder of lamb, cut into chunks
Salt and pepper
1 tbsp plain flour
Leaves from 4 or 5 sprigs thyme
1 tbsp oil
750g onions, thinly sliced
1kg potatoes – preferably King Edwards – peeled and
fairly thinly sliced
25g melted butter
150ml chicken stock

METHOD
- Preheat the oven to 180°C, gas mark 4.
- Season the lamb with salt and pepper and dust it with the flour. Put it in a dish about 20cm in diameter, with fairly high sides – about 10cm. Sprinkle the thyme leaves over the lamb.
- Heat the oil in a pan and cook the onions, without colouring, until they begin to soften. Put the onions on top of the lamb.
- Put the sliced potatoes in a bowl with some salt and pepper and pour over the melted butter. Carefully coat the potatoes with the butter, then arrange them on top of the onions, using the best-shaped slices for the final layer.
- Add the stock and cover the dish with foil. Cook for 30 minutes at the preheated temperature, then turn down the oven to 140°C, gas mark 1, and cook for a further 2 hours.
- Take the cover off the dish and increase the temperature to 200°C, gas mark 6. Cook for 30 minutes or so, until the top layer is golden brown.

- Hot pot is traditionally served with beetroot or red cabbage – why not try the recipe for red cabbage on page 152?

HONEY AND LEMON THYME ICE CREAM

I inherited this recipe from my sister. It is just sublime! She used honey from her own bees, which fed on a whole range of different flowers but obviously any honey will do. You can use an ice cream machine if you have one, but my sister did it the old-fashioned way and it was gorgeously creamy.

INGREDIENTS
500ml whole milk (don't use skimmed or semi-skimmed)
10 or so sprigs lemon thyme
500ml double cream
200g honey
5 egg yolks

METHOD
- Heat the milk and lemon thyme in a pan until just below boiling. Take off the heat and allow the thyme to infuse for about 10 minutes.
- Strain the milk into a heat-proof bowl and add half the cream, and the honey and egg yolks.
- Place the bowl over a pan of simmering water and stir constantly until the mixture is thick enough to coat the back of a spoon. Do not allow the mixture to get too hot, or you will end up with posh sweet scrambled eggs!
- Remove from the heat, add the rest of the cream and strain into a shallow freezer-proof dish. (If you have an ice cream maker, just follow the manufacturer's instructions.) Allow to cool, then refrigerate for a couple of hours before putting it in the freezer.
- After three hours or so, take it out and give the mixture a good stir to break up the ice crystals. For a smooth consistency, repeat this process every hour until it is the texture you want. If you don't have time, don't worry, but you will end up with a granita-type ice cream, which will taste just as good.

Winter savory
Satureja montana

Type of plant	Hardy, semi-evergreen perennial
Height and spread	20cm/30cm
Best position	Full sun
Soil	Poor, well drained
Method of propagation	Seed, inside in the early growing season; semi-ripe cuttings
Part of plant used	Leaves

In my opinion, winter savory deserves to be more widely grown. It is every bit as flavourful as thyme, and if grown in a sheltered position keeps its leaves for a good part of the dormant season. It requires the same sort of growing conditions as summer savory, but being a perennial it will come back year after year. You may find it gets a bit straggly if you don't use many sprigs of it in your cooking, but you can trim it back occasionally to keep it in shape.

Winter savory is more peppery than its summer cousin, and being a robust herb it can withstand some heat, so is ideal for warming winter dishes. Here are a couple of recipes which I turn to when we fancy something a little different: the first is for Jerusalem artichokes, which are becoming more readily available in some supermarkets; the second is for a home-made version of an old favourite – baked beans, the ingredients for which are available just about everywhere!

JERUSALEM ARTICHOKES WITH WINTER SAVORY

Jerusalem artichokes are not artichokes, nor do they have anything to do with Jerusalem! The 'artichoke' bit comes from the fact that when Samuel Champlain, the founder of Quebec, came across them in his travels around Cape Cod, where native Americans were growing them, he described them as having 'the taste of artichokes': that is, the flavour of the hearts of European globe artichokes. The Jerusalem part is said to be derived from the fact that the plant was described by John de Franqueville, a seventeenth-century French merchant, as a girasol, a plant whose flowers turn with the sun. Girasol quickly changed into Jerusalem, and there we have it!

Jerusalem artichokes are delicious but they have an unfortunate side-effect in some people. John Goodyer, a seventeenth-century botanist, describes it quite bluntly: 'which way so ever they be dressed and eaten, they stir and cause a filthy loathsome stinking wind'. But there is a remedy! The herb savory is renowned for being an aid to digestion, so by pairing it with Jerusalem artichokes, the forecast may be a little less windy!

The edible part of the Jerusalem artichoke is the knobbly tuber, which can be harvested throughout the dormant season, when winter savory is still available. This method of cooking them really brings out their nutty flavour and is delicious served with chicken or roast game.

INGREDIENTS
30g butter
650g Jerusalem artichokes, peeled and halved
45g pancetta or similar ham, cut into strips
150ml water
1 tbsp winter savory, chopped
Salt and pepper

METHOD
- Melt the butter in a thick-bottomed pan, large enough to take the artichokes in one layer. Add the artichokes and ham and fry for about 3 minutes.
- Add the water, half the savory, and seasoning, cover tightly and cook over a low heat for 30–40 minutes. Check occasionally to make sure that there is sufficient liquid to prevent boiling dry.
- When the artichokes are cooked there should be a very thin layer of liquid left (if there is too much, remove the artichokes and reduce the liquid).
- Add the remaining savory to the pan and turn the artichokes so that they are coated in the savory and remaining liquid.

BAKED BEANS WITH WINTER SAVORY

I like tinned baked beans on toast. But I absolutely love home-made baked beans on thick, wholemeal toast made from home-made bread. Sometimes this comfort food just hits the spot like no other – not even a bar of chocolate!

INGREDIENTS

400g dried haricot beans (or 4 x 400g cans of haricot beans)

3 tbsp olive oil

2 onions, finely chopped

150g pancetta, finely chopped

2 cloves garlic, crushed

230g can chopped tomatoes

250ml passata

2 tbsp dark muscovado sugar

3 tbsp cider or white wine vinegar

1 tbsp winter savory, finely chopped

METHOD

- Soak the beans overnight. Then drain them and put them in a large saucepan. Cover the beans with water and bring to the boil. Simmer for about 45 minutes until they are tender. Drain and set aside. If you are using canned, pre-cooked beans, drain and rinse the beans and go straight to the next step.
- Preheat the oven to 150°C, gas mark 2.
- Heat the oil in a large flameproof and ovenproof casserole, add the onions and pancetta and cook for about 8 minutes until the onions soften slightly.
- Add the garlic, chopped tomatoes, passata, sugar, vinegar and beans. Add 400ml water and bring to simmering point.
- Cover and cook in the oven for about 1½ hours, or until the beans are very tender and you have a lovely, thick sauce.

Collections of robust herbs

Some of the robust culinary herbs are traditionally grouped together, and you will often come across these in recipes. The main two are *bouquet garni* and *herbes de Provence*.

Bouquet garni

A *bouquet garni* is little more than a selection of herbs tied together and popped into the pot during cooking – but it sounds so much more in French. The idea is to get a balance of flavours so that no one herb dominates; this blend will then complement the other ingredients in your casserole, stew or soup. In case you're thinking that you have to start experimenting with a whole herb gardenful of specimens, take heart, because the hard work has been done by generations of competent cooks who have tacitly agreed on just the right basic combination.

The herbs that make up your *bouquet garni* have to be hearty enough to impart flavour as well as withstand the cooking time; and if you are picking them fresh from the garden they have to be robust enough to survive winter conditions. These two aspects go hand in hand, since the herbs we are using all have their essential oils tucked away in sturdy foliage, and this will be released during slow cooking; and the plants themselves are hardy and evergreen.

The classic and simplest *bouquet garni*, which you can use for any type of meat or vegetable dish, consists of a bay leaf, one or two sprigs of thyme, and three or four sprigs of parsley: make sure that you use the stems of the parsley as well as the leaves, since most of the flavour is in the stems. This trio of bay, thyme and parsley has stood the test of time and is perfectly adequate on its own, but if you feel adventurous you can add extra herbs to suit the type of ingredient you are cooking.

For vegetarian dishes, the classic *bouquet garni* is hard to beat; if you are using meat, though, and you want to bring out the flavour of your dishes even more, adapt your *bouquet garni* to suit the type of meat you are using.

- For pork, try adding some sage.
- For poultry, you could add a sprig of rosemary, along with a strip of lemon zest.

- For lamb, a sprig of oregano is a flavoursome addition to the basic bunch.
- For beef and game, you could add winter savory.

If you want to add a little more flavour to all of them, include a short stalk of celery, and to keep the whole lot together wrap them up in a 'skin' of leek, before tying it with a piece of kitchen-grade string. Be sure to make the string long enough so that the end can be tied around the handle of the casserole dish or saucepan – this makes it so much easier to remove it at the end of the cooking time and avoids chasing it around with a spoon.

You can find dried herb-filled 'tea bags' in supermarkets that also go under the name of *bouquet garni*, but I would only use these as a last resort.

BOEUF BOURGUIGNON

There are probably as many recipes for *boeuf bourguignon* as there are French chefs, but this is the one I use. It's a classic recipe with the addition a 'standard' *bouquet garni*.

INGREDIENTS
1kg shin of beef or similar, cut into large chunks
2 tbsp seasoned flour
2 tbsp oil
20 very small onions or shallots
20 button mushrooms
1 large onion, peeled and chopped
80g fatty bacon, cut into chunks
1 *bouquet garni* – bay, parsley and thyme
3 cloves garlic, squashed not crushed
1 bottle red Burgundy
200ml stock

METHOD
- Coat the beef with the seasoned flour.
- Heat the oil in a heavy, flameproof casserole dish. Brown the meat on all sides. Remove the meat and set aside.
- Add the small onions to the casserole dish and brown them. Remove and set aside. Do the same with the mushrooms.
- Add the chopped onion and the bacon to the casserole dish and cook until the onions are soft but not too brown.
- Return the beef to the casserole dish, together with the herbs, garlic, wine and stock. Bring to simmering point and simmer very gently for 1½ hours, or until the meat is tender. Don't let it boil.
- Add the small onions and mushrooms and cook for a further 30 minutes.

HERB AND GARLIC STOCK

You can use this stock, made from the herbs of a classic *bouquet garni* plus some garlic, as the base for many delicious soups. It's simple to make, and the intensity of flavour from so few ingredients is always surprising.

INGREDIENTS
1ltr water
1 large bulb or 2 small bulbs garlic
2 bay leaves
2 sprigs thyme
2 sprigs parsley
Salt and pepper

METHOD
- Bring the water to the boil.
- Separate the garlic into cloves, peel them and add them to the water along with the herbs and some salt. Cover and simmer for about 20 minutes.
- Take off the heat and strain. Add pepper to taste.

Herbes de Provence

Little terracotta pots or brightly coloured fabric sacks containing this collection of dried herbs from the limestone upland of the Midi can be found in many a French market. Which herbs should be included in the mixture is hotly debated but the general consensus is that four robust herbs are vital: oregano, rosemary, sage and thyme. (I have seen some *herbes de Provence* containing fennel, crushed bay and even lavender.) If you want to be true to tradition this is the one time that you should use dried herbs; nevertheless, I still like to use fresh. Any Mediterranean dish will be enhanced by the judicious addition of some of these highly aromatic herbs, but I particularly like to include them in a very simple fresh tomato sauce, made with onions, garlic and tomatoes.

ROAST DUCK WITH HERBES DE PROVENCE

I read somewhere that only one herb at a time should be used with duck, thyme being the favourite. But while on holiday in France I had a simple dinner of roast leg of duck with *herbes de Provence* and zest of orange. It was delicious.

INGREDIENTS
4 tbsp chopped *herbes de Provence*
(oregano, rosemary, sage and thyme)
Grated zest of 1 orange
Salt and pepper
4 duck legs

METHOD
- Preheat the oven to 180°C, gas mark 4.
- Mix together the herbs, orange zest, salt and pepper.
- Carefully ease the skin of the duck away from the flesh, without removing it, and gently push the herb mixture into the gap, distributing it evenly. Smooth the skin back and prick the legs with a skewer to allow any fat to escape during cooking.
- Place the legs on a rack over a roasting tin and cook for 20 minutes.
- Turn the oven down to 160°C, gas mark 3, and cook for a further 40 minutes or so until the duck is cooked through. The flavour of the herbs will have permeated the duck and the skin will be crispy.

What robust herbs go with what ingredient?

We looked at what delicate herbs go with what ingredient in the previous chapter. When it comes to robust herbs, most of us know that certain combinations work well because we are aware of traditional pairings, like sage with pork. But are there any robust herbs that go well with duck, or eggs, or even fruit? The answer is yes, there are! So here I start with the type of ingredient and recommend which herbs would enhance the flavours even more. You can then experiment with different combinations until you find one that you like.

Meat, fish, eggs and dairy

- *Beef* – bay, chervil, garlic, horseradish, hyssop, oregano, parsley, thyme, winter savory
- *Lamb* – bay, garlic, hyssop, oregano, parsley, rosemary, thyme, winter savory
- *Pork* – bay, chervil, garlic, hyssop, parsley, sage, winter savory
- *Chicken and turkey* – bay, celery leaf, chervil, garlic, hyssop, parsley, rosemary, thyme
- *Duck and goose* – bay, celery leaf, garlic, oregano, parsley, rosemary, sage, thyme
- *White fish* – bay, chervil, parsley (white fish generally requires a short cooking time so normally I wouldn't use a robust herb with it – but these are the exceptions)
- *Oily fish* – bay, chervil, garlic, oregano, parsley, thyme (oily fish such as mackerel can cope with the stronger flavours of some of the robust herbs)
- *Eggs, milk, cheese* – bay, chervil, lavender, oregano, parsley

Vegetables

- *Root vegetables* (carrots, celeriac, kohlrabi, Jerusalem artichokes, potatoes, parsnips, swede, turnip; I include leeks in this group, too) – bay, celery leaf, horseradish, parsley, rosemary, sage, thyme, winter savory
- *Brassicas* (e.g. cabbage, cauliflower, broccoli, kale) – parsley, rosemary, sage, thyme, winter savory
- *Legumes* (e.g. peas, beans, mange-tout) – chervil, oregano, parsley, rosemary, sage, thyme, winter savory
- *Cucurbits* (e.g. cucumber, courgette, squash) – chervil, oregano, parsley, thyme, winter savory

Salads

- *Leaves* – celery leaf, chervil, parsley
- *Tomatoes* – bay, chervil, oregano, parsley, thyme

Desserts

You may not immediately think of using herbs with desserts, but some robust herbs lend themselves to sweet concoctions, particularly if the recipes contain fruit – bay, hyssop, rosemary.

And Finally

I hope that by the time you read this you will be confident enough to have a go at growing your own herbs and, more than that, using them in your own kitchen. There are herbs to be had throughout the year; many of them lend themselves to seasonal use, as I hope I have shown here.

If you catch the 'herb bug' you can have a go at growing and using all thirty herbs that I have suggested – but even these are just a drop in the herbal ocean: there are scores, perhaps hundreds, more that you could try. But even if you only pick out the ones you know you will use most often, I can almost guarantee that it won't be long before your collection expands. The more you grow herbs and the more you use them in the kitchen, the more you will appreciate their flavour, versatility, and ability to complement and enhance other ingredients.

So grab a garden fork and get growing, and a kitchen fork and get cooking, and see how you can transform your garden and your cuisine with these most useful of all plants.

Appendix 1
Latin Names of Chosen Herbs

English common name	Latin name	Other common name(s)
Basil	*Ocimum basilicum*	Sweet basil
Bay	*Laurus nobilis*	Sweet laurel
Bergamot	*Monarda didyma*	Bee balm
Borage	*Borago officinalis*	Starflower
Celery leaf	*Apium graveolens*	Wild celery, par-cel
Chervil	*Anthriscus cerefolium*	
Chives	*Allium schoenoprasum*	
Coriander	*Coriandrum sativum*	Cilantro
Dill	*Anethum graveolens*	Dillweed
Fennel	*Foeniculum vulgare*	Sweet fennel
Garlic	*Allium sativum*	
Horseradish	*Armoracia rusticana*	
Hyssop	*Hyssopus officinalis*	
Lavender	*Lavandula* sp.	
Lemon balm	*Melissa officinalis*	Melissa, bee balm
Lemon grass	*Cymbopogon citratus*	
Lemon verbena	*Aloysia triphylla*	Vervain
Lovage	*Levisticum officinale*	Love parsley
Marjoram – sweet	*Origanum majorana*	Knotted marjoram
Mint – garden	*Mentha spicata*	Lamb mint
Mint – apple	*Mentha suaveolens*	
Myrtle	*Myrtus communis*	
Oregano	*Origanum vulgare*	
Parsley	*Petroselinum crispum*	Persil
Parsley – French	*Petroselinum crispum* 'French'	Flat-leaf parsley

English common name	Latin name	Other common name(s)
Rosemary	*Rosmarinus officinalis*	
Sage	*Salvia officinalis*	Common sage, garden sage
Sage – golden	*Salvia officinalis* 'Icterina'	
Sage – purple	*Salvia officinalis* Purpurascens Group	
Summer savory	*Satureja hortensis*	Bean herb
Sweet cicely	*Myrrhis odorata*	Anise
Sweet marjoram	*Origanum majorana*	Marjoram
Tarragon – French	*Artemisia dracunculus*	
Thyme – common	*Thymus vulgaris*	Garden thyme
Thyme – broad-leaf	*Thymus pulegioides*	
Thyme – lemon	*Thymus citriodorus*	
Winter savory	*Satureja montana*	

Where and When to Sow Herb Seeds

Herb	Sow inside	Sow outside	Late growing season	Early growing season
Basil	✓			✓
Bay	✓		✓	
Bergamot	✓			✓
Borage	✓	✓		✓
Celery leaf		✓	✓	
Chervil		✓	✓	
Chives	✓	✓		✓
Coriander		✓		✓
Dill		✓		✓
Fennel		✓	✓	
Hyssop	✓			✓
Lavender	✓			✓
Lemon balm	✓			
Lemon grass	✓			
Lovage	✓		✓	
Oregano	✓			✓
Parsley		✓	✓	
Rosemary	✓			✓
Sage	✓			✓
Summer savory	✓			✓
Sweet cicely		✓	✓	
Sweet marjoram	✓			✓
Thyme	✓		✓	
Winter savory	✓	✓	✓	

Appendix 3

What Type of Cutting is Suitable for Which Herb

Herb	Softwood	Type of cutting Semi-ripe	Root
Bay		✓	
Bergamot		✓	✓
Horseradish			✓
Hyssop	✓		
Lavender	✓		
Lemon balm	✓		
Lemon verbena		✓	
Mint	✓		✓
Myrtle	✓		
Oregano	✓		
Rosemary		✓	
Sage		✓	
Sweet cicely			✓
Sweet marjoram	✓		
Tarragon	✓		✓
Thyme		✓	
Winter savory		✓	

Useful Addresses and Websites

Author's website
www.the beegarden.co.uk
Also see author's page on www.amazon.co.uk

Herb related
Nearly all good garden centres and nurseries sell herb plants and/or
seeds. Here are a few specialist nurseries, however, should you fail to
find what you want locally. Please contact them first to find out if
and when they are open to the public before making a special
journey – some are just mail order.

The Garden Studio
www.thegarden-studio.co.uk
01772 812672
Specialist perennial nursery, Lancashire – a wide range of herbs are
available. Also offer short courses on herbs and other subjects.

Downderry Nursery
www.downderry-nursery.co.uk
01732 810081
Lavender and rosemary specialist, Kent.

Hooksgreen Herbs
www.hooksgreenherbs.com
07977 883810
Herb growers, Staffordshire.

Iden Croft Herbs
www.uk-herbs.com
01580 891432
Herb growers, Kent – beautiful garden.

Jekka's Herb Farm
www.jekkasherbfarm.com
01454 418878
Organic herb specialist, South Gloucestershire.

Suffolk Herbs
www.kingseeds.com
01376 572456
Supplier of herb seeds, Essex.

Societies
The Herb Society
www.herbsociety.org.uk
0845 491 8699

Other websites of interest
Alice Shields
www.alice-shields.co.uk
Beautiful ceramics – including herb labels.

Index of Recipes

Sweet dishes and desserts

Index